Mapping *The Faerie Queene*

GARLAND STUDIES IN THE RENAISSANCE
VOLUME 3
GARLAND REFERENCE LIBRARY OF THE HUMANITIES
VOLUME 1835

GARLAND STUDIES IN THE RENAISSANCE
RAYMOND B. WADDINGTON, *Series Editor*

RUBENS AND THE ROMAN CIRCLE
Studies of the First Decade
by Frances Huemer

READING THE RENAISSANCE
Culture, Poetics, and Drama
by Jonathan Hart

THE EXPULSION OF THE JEWS
1492 and After
by Raymond B. Waddington
and Arthur H. Williamson

OUR ACCUSTOMED DISCOURSE
ON THE ANTIQUE
Cesare Gonzaga and Gerolamo Garimberto, Two Renaissance Collectors of Greco-Roman Art
by Clifford Malcolm Brown, with
the collaboration of Anna Maria Lorenzoni

MAPPING *THE FAERIE QUEENE*
Quest Structures and the World of the Poem
by Wayne Erickson

Mapping *The Faerie Queene*
Quest Structures and the World of the Poem

Wayne Erickson

Garland Publishing, Inc.
New York and London
1996

Library of Congress Cataloging-in-Publication Data

Erickson, Wayne.
Mapping the faerie queene : quest structures and the world of the poem / Wayne Erickson.
p. cm. — (Garland reference library of the humanities ; vol. 1835. Garland studies in the Renaissance ; v. 3)
Includes bibliographical references and index.
ISBN 0-8153-1658-5 (alk. paper)
1. Spenser, Edmund, 1552?–1599. Faerie queene. 2. Epic poetry, English—History and criticism. 3. Knights and knighthood in literature. 4. Geographical myths in literature. 5. Geography in literature. 6. Quests in literature. I. Title. II. Series: Garland reference library of the humanities ; vol. 1835. III. Series: Garland reference library of the humanities. Garland studies in the Renaissance ; vol. 3.
PR2358.E75 1996
821'.3—dc20 95-50636
CIP

Printed on acid-free, 250-year-life paper
Manufactured in the United States of America

For my parents, who always let me go.

(Entire affection hateth nicer hands)

Contents

Acknowledgments ix
Introduction: Mapping Multiplicity 3
I. Epic and History 19
II. Epic and Romance 41
III. The Epic World of *The Faerie Queene* 59
1. Faeryland: The Verisimilar Fiction 60
2. The Larger World of the Poem 65
The Epic Cosmos 65
Terrestrial Geography 68
Local Political Geography: The British Isles and Western Europe 71
Temporal Geography 72
Eden lands, Cleopolis, and Mercilla's Court 76
3. Faeryland and the Larger World 79
IV. Britain and the Epic Quests 87
1. Britain and Faeryland 87
2. The Quests from Cleopolis 95
3. The Quests from Britain 99
Epilogue: Stranded in Faeryland 119
Bibliography 131
Index 145

Acknowledgments

For advice, assistance, encouragement, and other kinds of support, I thank Marcy Alexander, Patricia Bryan, Patrick Bryant, Edith Buchanan, Virginia Spencer Carr, Peter Chase, Morris Eaves, Brett Erickson, Caitlin Erickson, Ruth Erickson, Robert O. Evans, Cheryl Fresch, A.C. Hamilton, A. Kent Hieatt, Wendy Jones, Leigh Kirkland, Phyllis Korper, Marc Montefusco, Michael O'Connell, Rob Poss, James Poulakos, George Pullman, Ginger Pyron, Thomas P. Roche, Jr., William A. Sessions, Paul Schmidt, Dorothy Sussman, Jim Threlkeld, Raymond B. Waddington, and Portia Weiskel. Errors, omissions, and infelicities are, of course, my own.

MAPPING *THE FAERIE QUEENE*

Introduction
Mapping Multiplicity

This book maps the geography of *The Faerie Queene*'s setting, outlining and analyzing the various places that compose the world of the poem. Most conspicuous among these places is Faeryland, the time-inclusive, predominantly allegorical world of chivalric adventure where most of the action occurs. Spenser situates Faeryland within a multiform fictional universe, including a syncretic epic cosmos stretching from heaven and the abode of the classical deities to demonic underground realms and a complex terrestrial setting comprising a generalized fallen earth and a specific spatial and temporal political geography. My emphasis falls especially upon the political or historical geography, which depicts several distinct places and times, several perspectives on Tudor history manifesting innovative variations on the traditional heroic setting in political and religious history: a multivalent representation of religious history, myth, and legend in the kingdom of "*Eden* lands"[1] (1.7.43, 11.1–2; 2.1.1); a sixth-century heroic and legendary setting in Arthurian Britain (Wales and Cornwall), from which the Saxon Redcrosse and all the Briton knights enter Faeryland (1.9.4, 10.65–6; 3.2.18, 3.26–7,62); a sixteenth-century theater of controversial political and juridical action in the land of Mercilla, gateway to international conflict in Ireland and Western Europe (5.10.7, 12.2–4,10); and a richly allusive sixteenth-century and prophetic historical matrix at the court of Gloriana in Cleopolis (1.10.58–9; 2.2.39–43). By situating Faeryland within the larger spatial, temporal, and ontological setting, this book challenges the prevailing critical assumption that Faeryland is coextensive with the world of the poem; in doing so, it provides a widened context for interpretations of the major quest structures, demonstrates the breadth and flexibility of Spenser's historical imagination, and highlights the interplay among his various historiographical, political, and generic representations.

Although Spenser manipulates and merges genres in a variety of ways and consistently controverts the efficacy of monolithic and dualistic interpretive models, one preliminary means of placing *The Faerie Queene*'s setting within a critical context is to engage issues of genre. The distinction Spenser draws between Faeryland and places outside of it—that is, between the respective subject matters and modes of representation characteristic of these locales—is roughly analogous to the Renaissance distinction between, respectively, romance and epic or, alternatively, between romance epic and heroic epic. From this perspective, the places outside Faeryland are variously analogous to Homer's Troy and Ithaca, Virgil's Latium and Rome, Ariosto's Paris, Tasso's Jerusalem, the king's court in chivalric romance, and the waking state in dream vision; likewise, Faeryland's analogues include the worlds of Odysseus's and Aeneas's wanderings and the multitudinous medieval and Renaissance variations on the forest of chivalric adventure, the mental landscape of dream vision, and marvelous locales generally.

While helpful and fairly accurate, the romance/epic distinction between Faeryland and the larger world of the poem should be understood within the context of Spenser's own remarks on his poem's genre. When he advertises his poem in the Letter to Ralegh, Spenser pointedly eschews conventional terminology for naming narrative genre—epic, heroic, romance—and instead invents his own, which emphasizes allegory and history.[2] He writes, he says, "a continued Allegory, or darke conceit" that he has "coloured with an historicall fiction" because such a subject matter is "most plausible and pleasing," the history supplying the plausibility, and thus the applause of those who distrust fiction, and the fiction supplying the pleasure necessary to attract a national audience. And he calls not only Homer and Virgil but also Ariosto and Tasso his fellow "Poets historicall." Here, in his public voice, Spenser admits the allegorical and fictional nature of his creation while emphasizing its moral and historical character, thereby implicitly stressing his poem's austere epic dignity and his own epic aspirations. He insists that the philosopher's "precepts" are "deliuered plainly" and that it is allegory that obscures or clouds the moral ideas; similarly, he refuses to question the exemplary moral power of historical truth, stating that he introduces "an historicall fiction"—"the historye of king Arthure"—because most readers enjoy a fictionalized account of history, "rather for variety of matter, then for profite of the ensample." Moral and political "doctrine" may be more "delightfull and pleasing to commune sence" when "clowdily enwrapped in

Allegoricall deuises," and history may be more "pleasing" to a larger audience when "coloured" by fiction; but, in both cases, the poetical adornments are mere "showes," superficial attractions and distractions, since the moral "ensample" inheres in the historical record as the doctrinal "rule" inheres in the philosophical discourse. By inventing his own generic terminology, stressing moral and historical truth, and displaying a condescending attitude toward allegory and fiction, Spenser uses the Letter to Ralegh to assert implicitly his poem's epic status while downplaying its associations with romance. In the poem, he creates a setting and quest structures consistent with his publicly stated intention.

The universe of *The Faerie Queene* includes a horizontal dimension of spatial and temporal geography and a vertical dimension of topographical and cosmological geography. The horizontal—the earthly setting in the fallen world—intersects the vertical—an ontological spectrum extending from heaven to hell—on the plain in Faeryland where much of the action of the poem occurs. In general, vertical shifts in the setting—up a mountain, down into a valley or cave, up or down into a building—reflect changes in the ontological status of the events portrayed, usually accompanied by an increase in allegorical intensity roughly proportional to the distance of a particular setting from the plain. At the upper limit of Faeryland lie what C.S. Lewis named the "allegorical core[s]," such places as the Mount of Contemplation, Alma's castle, the Garden of Adonis, the Temple of Venus, Isis Church, and Mount Acidale.[3] At the lower limit lie their demonic counterparts, such places as the dungeon of Orgoglio; the caves of Error, Despair, Ate, Malengin, and the Brigants; and the houses of Mammon and Busirane. The narrative of Faeryland unfolds between these vertical poles; any place higher than the Mount of Contemplation (1.10.53–9) or deeper than the house of Mammon (2.7.56–7) exists, respectively, in the heavens or in hell.

Descent into hell proper—that is, travel across one of the four rivers of Hades—occurs at least once (1.5.31–41), and probably on two other occasions (1.1.39; 4.2.47). Spenser's heaven is a syncretic creation with Christian, classical, and astrological associations. The divine Christian world enters the narrative when Redcrosse views the New Jerusalem (1.10.55–7) and when an angel descends to protect Guyon after he faints (2.8.5–8). Venus leaves her "heauenly hous" to search the earth for Cupid (3.6.12–16); Cymoent ascends "Vnto the shinie heauen" to bring back Apollo to cure Marinell (4.12.25); Astraea returns to her "euerlasting place" in heaven (as the constellation Virgo) when she retreats from the fallen earth (5.1.11); and Mutabilitie travels "To *Ioues* high Palace" (7.6.7–8,23).

Spenser ties his poem to national history by making Faeryland part of a larger political geography. Faeryland occupies the political space of Elizabethan England or "Logris land" (2.Proem.4; 4.11.36); across the sea to the west is the land of "fayre *Irena*," Artegall's destination (5.12.10); across the sea to the east is the land of "*Belge*," where Arthur goes on Mercilla's behalf (5.10.7); directly to the north, across the Tweed, lies Picteland or Albany (2.10.14; 4.12.36; 6.12.4); and to the southwest, across the Dee, the Severn, and the Tamar, lie the Celtic lands of Wales and Cornwall, the Britain of *The Faerie Queene* (2.10.14; 4.11.31,39). From Britain, the Briton knights enter Faeryland: Arthur travels from North Wales (1.9.4–6) and Britomart from South Wales (3.2.18; 3.3.62); Artegall and Redcrosse are brought to Faeryland as changelings, Artegall from Cornwall (3.3.26–7) and Redcrosse, the only Saxon hero in the poem, from somewhere in "*Britane* land" (1.10.65). The temporal dimension of this political geography allows the poem a multiple relation to history: the time in the Low Countries, France, and Ireland (except in the *Cantos of Mutabilitie*) is the sixteenth century; the time in Britain is the sixth century; and specific historical references relate Cleopolis and Mercilla's court to Elizabethan London. Eden, distanced in space and time, is associated with its traditional setting (1.7.43) and with the time of biblical myth.

In Faeryland, where various historical, legendary, and mythical times coexist, past, present, and future must be treated as relative, not absolute, terms. Since Spenser frees Faeryland from the burden of any particular time, he can use it to coordinate the historical circumstances of the epic quests, the political and religious events that occur and are destined to occur in the places that compose the political geography surrounding Faeryland. The major quests originate either in sixth-century Britain or in sixteenth-century Cleopolis. At her annual feast in Cleopolis, Gloriana assigns to the Faery knights, Guyon and Calidore, moral and social quests that take place entirely within Faeryland; to the knights of Britain, Redcrosse and Artegall, she assigns religious and political quests that conclude outside Faeryland, the one in Eden lands and the other in sixteenth-century Ireland. The quests of Arthur and Britomart emerge directly from sixth-century Britain, a heroic realm of political conflict and mimetic realism, and are destined to conclude in Cleopolis and Britain, respectively. Together, the quests create a pattern of temporal mediations among sixteenth-century English, sixth-century British, biblical, and prophetic history.

Spenser creates three parallel epic quests representing three temporal perspectives on Tudor history, and he ties the quests to Cleopolis, Britain, and Eden, which form a political and religious historical frame around the moral, erotic, and social allegory of Faeryland. Upon their return to Britain, Britomart and Artegall, like Aeneas, would begin to build a nation out of chaos; they would establish the Tudor line as Aeneas had established the

Augustan. Upon reaching Cleopolis, Arthur would, by serving and marrying Gloriana, initiate the prophetic nation of Tudor legend. The realization of Arthur's quest would have taken Anchises' prophecy to Aeneas one step further, beyond the poet's own time into the future of an apocalyptic third Troy. Redcrosse, whose quest parallels in religious history that of Arthur in political history, is destined to return to Eden lands where, by marrying Una, he would establish the redeemed earth. Spenser creates an innovative political and ontological geography capable of accommodating the momentous heroic epic he never finished writing.

Critics who discuss the setting of *The Faerie Queene* almost invariably treat Faeryland as equivalent to the world of the poem, arguing or assuming that all the action of the poem occurs in Faeryland, that Spenser, to use Jonathan Goldberg's phrase, "locates his text" in a place or state of being he names Faeryland.[4] Despite its shortcomings, the basic assumption persists, sometimes accompanied by value judgments concerning the poem's genre that mimic Italian Renaissance attacks leveled at Ariosto: that the poem is *only* a romance and therefore per se less valuable than if it were epic. More often, of course, modern critics celebrate the poem as a gloriously successful allegorical romance or romance epic while nonetheless admitting that it lacks certain traditional components of epic, among them a firm foundation in history or the "real" world. According to this line of reasoning, Spenser breaks with epic tradition by failing to bring his narrative into direct contact with quotidian reality; specifically, since Spenser supposedly sets the entire action of his poem in an imagined world, he fails to relate his historical argument to representations of actual places such as Troy, Ithaca, Carthage, Latium, Paris, or Jerusalem, which serve as authoritatively legitimate gateways into the fiction. The general emphasis of this prevailing point of view is not wholly inaccurate; unlike most other writers of heroic or romance narrative, Spenser sets most of the action of his poem in an invented world. But the fact remains that he does situate Faeryland within a recognizable universe; and he supplies—in the epic cosmos and in the transparent representations of specific times, places, and events that frame Faeryland—the "situation," "ordinary beginning," "known world," and "real geography and history" that, respectively, Lewis, Tillyard, Roche, and Murrin find lacking.[5] Thus, the critical assumption of identity between Faeryland and the setting of the poem betrays a significant factual error which, by narrowing the scope of the setting, limits an understanding of the ways Spenser ties his poem to history and epic tradition and the ways he coordinates the heroic and romance aspects of the major quests within his multiform narrative world.

Even those critics who note, here and there and usually in passing, that such places as Eden, Wales, Cleopolis, Mercilla's and Gloriana's courts, and the sites of historical action in Book 5 are distanced and distinguished from Faeryland proper do not put the geography together.[6] Instead, they almost invariably end up either ignoring the significance of the distinctions, comparing Faeryland exclusively to one of these places (usually "Britain"), or collapsing the multiform world into some comprehensive idea of Faeryland. In the process, they soften and simplify the hard edge and complexity of Spenser's plural analysis, particularly when they yoke an inclusive idea of Faeryland to exclusive terms such as *ideal*, *prelapsarian*, *Elysian*, *golden*, or *green*. These critical procedures tend to generate dualistic interpretive models, including those commonplace ones that set the ideal or fictional world of Faeryland (meaning the whole poem) over against the real or historical world outside the poem. Such models, while minimally useful as initial entries into interpretation, distort *The Faerie Queene*'s fictional world and inhibit a recognition of its multiplicity.

Similarly reductive strategies manifest themselves in the more radical versions of recent historicist theory. To bluntly simplify a complex theoretical paradigm: if all human beings are nothing but "cultural artifacts,"[7] and the texts they produce nothing but cultural artifacts once removed; and if culture is a function of an ideology conceived to sustain—in Elizabethan England—autocratic political power, then all texts consciously or unconsciously reproduce in order to sustain that power. In other words, since ideological systems clone texts, those texts—and the parts thereof—differ only by degree from one another. The critical practice that endorses this model must disallow the relatively qualitative distinctions I see Spenser drawing between Faeryland and the places outside of it and among the various places within and outside of it: furthermore, such critical practice, which asserts the sovereign power of political ideology, must also disallow the relative autonomy of actions in a Faeryland that Spenser distances from external political control.

Contemporary historicist critics, while challenging all literary critics to face and assess their theoretical assumptions, often seem inadequately cognizant of the ways in which their own critical procedures participate in some of the same limitations and distortions they expose in the procedures of others. Specifically, they endorse monolithic and dualistic interpretive models formally, if not always materially, analogous to those they disparage in earlier critics, models equally incapable of accommodating the multiplicity of *The Faerie Queene*'s setting. They offer helpful critiques of widely influential literary historical paradigms such as E.M.W. Tillyard's "Elizabethan world picture,"[8] which they convincingly expose as politically motivated by postwar conservatism, relatively ignorant of intertextual complexity, and reductive both as an expression of Renaissance cultural mythology and as a basis for literary interpretation. Yet the cultural model at the foundation of much contemporary historicist analysis of Renaissance texts, a model influenced by Foucault's Renaissance epistime, is an only slightly modified version of Tillyard's "world picture"; Tillyard's cultural paradigm—an orderly, coherent, hierarchical design—remains substantially unchanged, but its source and purpose alter radically: a providential design reflected in the faith of a people becomes a crass political maneuver aimed at containing and obliterating challenges to autocratic ideological dominion. An idealized Faeryland depicting displays of virtuous and heroic action thus becomes an equally monolithic representation of absolute political power. Such theoretical assumptions motivate Stephen Greenblatt to assert categorically that "*The Faerie Queene* is . . . wholly wedded to the autocratic ruler of the English state," that Spenser "loves" and "worships power," and that in celebrating and seeking to justify a "repellent political ideology" Spenser betrays his "passionate worship of imperialism."[9] These absolute pronouncements, in which theory negates alternate interpretations and sanctions intentional fallacy, betray the same tendency as those that present Faeryland, or the world of the poem, as a transparent reflection of an idealized Elizabethan culture.

Contemporary historicism offers a stimulating critique of traditional dualistic interpretive models, but the new models it proposes exhibit the same limitations that impair any dualistic critical strategy. Since historicist theory dismantles boundaries between kinds of cultural texts, it collapses distinctions between categories such as fact and fiction, real and ideal, and epic and romance. It replaces these with the dualities of power: absolutist ideology creates the "alien" or the "other" in order to contain or consume it;[10] the oppressed confront the oppressors and usually end up crushed beneath the heel of authority;[11] and art confronts ideology and ends up either embracing it, being coopted by it, or attempting a futile escape by retreating to the impotent margins of the text.[12] Interpretive choices remain nominally binary, though any fissures in the inexorable monolith of power tend to repair themselves quickly and effortlessly.

This severely condensed evaluation of a revisionist historicism informed by Marxist, anthropological, and linguistic theory demands qualification, particularly in light of recent critical reappraisals of its earlier excesses and the wide range of practical criticism currently being performed under the rubrics "new historicism" and "cultural materialism." Indeed, seminal new historicist documents have spawned a minor critical industry of supplemental and oppositional responses.[13] Cultural materialists, resisting a monolithic conception of ideology and exploiting cracks in the structures of power, allow some space for human agency both within criticism and within literary texts. Alan Sinfield argues "that the complexities of the power structure make it possible to envisage the literary text not necessarily as subversive, but as a site of contest, and [that] the distinctive location of the state servant might produce a critical perspective."[14] Within the new historicist camp itself, Louis Montrose suggests that "[e]very representation of power is also an appropriation of power,"[15] and Richard Helgerson, while asserting that the "kingdom/nation authorizes—indeed authors—the text/form," concedes that "the reverse is also true" and that "the individual writer" and various "discursive communities" participate in the production of texts.[16] Even Greenblatt has followed suit, admitting that he "grew increasingly uneasy with the monolithic entities that [his] work had posited."[17]

Within this more open and experimental historicist context, in which critics acknowledge the value of and their debts to older historical criticism, Spenser's multiform setting seems ripe for analysis. The various places that compose the setting of *The Faerie Queene* display a variety of historical, political, and historiographical perspectives on Tudor history that might be understood as reflecting the priorities and preoccupations of various Elizabethan "discursive communities." Furthermore, the geographical dimensions of the setting—Spenser's mapping of his fictional world—invite the kind of commentary that recent critics have devoted to other Renaissance cartographic and chorographic projects.[18] These matters lie somewhat beyond the scope of this book, which seeks primarily to describe the *Faerie Queene*'s multiform setting and to show how it enables Spenser's manipulations of history and genre. By exposing the poem's multiplicity, the book challenges historicist critics to consider a pluralist perspective and to revaluate their most persistent assumptions: that cultural power conditions and controls representation and interpretation; that all cultural negotiations are negotiations with power; that every human action is a cultural representation and therefore a cultural text; and that all textual production is political production and all actions within texts political actions.

The Faerie Queene solicits plural interpretations including but not limited to cultural ones. While cultural actions and identities might legitimately be defined as political, Spenser's text suggests that some determinants of actions and identities might exist below or beyond culture: that certain human experiences, certain acts of creation and participation, transcend ideology and embrace mysteries that thwart materialist interpretation. Cultural production vitally concerns Spenser, but other possible influences on human life also consume his interest. His poem displays his fascination with biology (including genetics and sex), chemistry (including alchemy, drugs, and humors), meteorology, astronomy and astrology, topographical and topological and ontological location, fate, fortune, the gods, magic, divine providence, change as a force of nature, and so on, not to mention inspiration, vision, prophecy, and imagination. Spenser opens up intellectual debate, suggests various—and variously imperfect—answers, and suspends conclusiveness, leaving readers, at their discretion, to formulate definitive solutions. This is how *The Faerie Queene* characteristically works, partly because Spenser provides multiple perspectives on the same issues and partly because of the nature of his allegorical method. An analogous relationship exists among the multiform nature of Spenser's setting, the polyphonic nature of his narrative, the interpenetrative nature of his characterizations, and the polysemous nature of his allegory: all demand an ongoing process of interpretation. One place, story, character, or allegorical signification suggests and spontaneously produces others in a continuous interpretive process that refines as it complicates meaning. The process is both linear (like epic) and cyclical (like romance), each element and interpretation leading to others while simultaneously circling back to reinterpret, qualify, and supplement what has come before.

Spenser introduces the process theoretically when, in the Letter to Ralegh, he calls his poem "a continued Allegory, or darke conceit." His allegory is "continued"—relatively continuous or constant throughout the poem—rather than sporadic like Ariosto's and Tasso's, and its meaning develops continuously, with interpretations of each element continued, conditioned, and expanded by the next.[19] The "conceit"—idea, extended metaphor, elaborate contrivance, startling comparison—is "darke" in that it is hidden, veiled, available only to an elite, and packed with esoteric significance; it is also "darke" in that it is ambiguous, allusive, full of meaning that awaits disclosure, awaits unpacking. The "good discipline"—ethical "precept" and historical "ensample"—that constitutes the didactic matter of the conceit is darkened, "coloured," "shadow[ed]," and "clowdily enwrapped" both to hide or obscure meaning and to disclose meaning or make it immediately, though always conditionally, available.[20] Thus, Spenser's allegory intimates a truth that it continuously defers. The poem stands ready to initiate allegorical interpretation, what Gordon Teskey calls the game of "interpretative play": "while the goal of interpretation is to eradicate all signifying difference in a motionless ideal, the very work of moving toward the ideal opens more spaces than it can close. The true purpose, therefore, of that increasingly problematic structure of meaning which we accumulate as we read is not to capture the truth but to engage us in further, and more powerful, interpretative play." Such play is neither purposeless nor vain; indeed, it functions as the process by which, according to the Letter to Ralegh, Spenser intends to "fashion" his readers "in vertuous and gentle discipline": readers are "to be morally changed not just by seeing examples of admirable conduct but by becoming engaged, through the play of interpretation, in the theory of virtue. Spenser's allegorical writing, like Dante's, fashions an intellectual habit."[21]

Although exclusive and stable dualistic models limit and distort interpretations of *The Faerie Queene*, the poem relentlessly produces terminological pairs, which serve as one means of initiating "interpretative play." They begin a process that develops in several ways: first, each of the two terms yields various significations that allow the terms to define each other in a variety of ways; second, the terms interpenetrate and overlap in ways that exploit their problematical identity or fluid interrelation rather than their stable difference; third, and perhaps most crucial, the terms define the ends of spectrums in which meaning resides at contestable points between the ends, an interpretive model made all the more complicated by the multiple significations associated with the terms at the ends. Plugging any set of terms into this paradigm produces the kind of polysemous meaning characteristic of the poem. For instance, one might consider, among dozens of possibilities, pairs such as faith/despair, temperance/wrath, love/lust, loving embrace/rape, love/hate, justice/mercy, gentle/common, strive/rest, nature/nurture, stability/change, male/female, and any number more. In my discussion of *The Faerie Queene*'s setting, certain pairs frequently appear: history/fiction, epic/romance, duty/desire, public/private, political/personal, Briton/Faery, allegorical/nonallegorical, queen/woman. All of these are, at once, distinct entities, interpenetrating and overlapping entities, and ends of spectrums.

Spenserians, particularly in recent years, have suggested various ways of accounting for, accommodating, and explaining *The Faerie Queene*'s copious meaning. For example, Kenneth Gross, following Paul Alpers, identifies one of Spenser's "'master tropes'" as *aporia*: "the figure entails the multiplication within a discourse of such a variety of alternative perspectives as to call into question, or at least to delay, any divisive choice among those alternatives." Patricia Parker suggests that "the Body of Errour, defeated in the opening episode, 'dilates' to fill out the remainder of the narrative." And Gordon Teskey constructs a poetics of allegory that opens volatile spaces for paradoxical coexistence and mutual assimilation of antiphrasis and polysemy.[22] My analysis of Spenser's multiform setting offers new models for approaching interpretation of *The Faerie Queene* consistent with the work of Gross, Parker, Teskey, and others who are discovering, or perhaps rediscovering, a skeptical, playful, perplexed, endlessly inventive, and, maybe, proto-Romantic Spenser who is something more than a pawn of political or linguistic ideological determinism. Within his plural setting—amid varied approaches to history, manipulations of genre, and intertextual play—Spenser stages inconclusive ideological warfare that defers all final solutions until "Short *Time*" shall "graunt [him] that Sabaoths sight" (7.8.1,2): until death or apocalypse swallows up all human wandering, all seeking after stability amid the unremitting flux of mortal life.

Chapter I of this study examines Spenser's assertions of epic status for *The Faerie Queene* in the context of Renaissance conceptions of the relationship between epic and history, focusing on Spenser's use of the Letter to Ralegh to advertise his poem's historical subject matter while ironically subverting simplistic distinctions between history and fiction. This discussion exposes Spenser's witty and innovative maneuverings by analyzing his defense of fiction and his response to the Elizabethan controversy surrounding the historicity of Arthur. The chapter concludes by examining Spenser's defense of his Faeryland setting in the Proem to Book 2. Chapter II turns from Spenser's embrace of epic to his embrace of romance, revaluating the relationship between *The Faerie Queene* and Italian romance epic in the light of Spenser's multiform setting and suggesting medieval sources in chivalric romance and dream vision for Spenser's setting and quest structures. Chapters III and IV outline and analyze the spatial, temporal, and ontological dimensions of *The Faerie Queene*'s setting, beginning with Faeryland and the epic cosmos and then moving on to the main subject: the terrestrial political geography that frames Faeryland, including, especially, Eden lands, Cleopolis, the land of Mercilla, and Britain. The last two sections of Chapter IV focus on distinctions between Briton and Faery quests and on quests originating in Britain and those originating in Cleopolis. The Epilogue explores the final actions of characters stranded in Faeryland amid dissolving boundaries. The book stresses Spenser's consciousness as epic poet to portray truth for his age as well as his desire to coordinate epic and romance quest structures within his multiform and thoroughly original fictional world.

Notes
Introduction

1. Edmund Spenser, *The Faerie Queene*, ed. A.C. Hamilton (London: Longman, 1977). All references to *The Faerie Queene* are to this edition and are cited in the text by book, canto, and stanza.

2. All references to Spenser's Letter to Ralegh ("A letter of the Authors expounding his whole intention in the course of this worke: which for that it giuith great light to the Reader, for the better vnderstanding is hereunto annexed.") are to *The Faerie Queene*, ed. Hamilton, 737–8. Since references to the Letter are explicit and since the text is only two pages long in Hamilton, I make no page citations.

3. C.S. Lewis, *The Allegory of Love: A Study in Medieval Tradition* (1936; rpt. New York: Oxford Univ. Press, 1963), 334.

4. Jonathan Goldberg, *Endlesse Worke: Spenser and the Structures of Discourse* (Baltimore: Johns Hopkins Univ. Press, 1981), 20.

5. Lewis, *Allegory*, 306. E.M.W. Tillyard, *The English Epic and Its Background*, (1954; rpt. Westport, CT: Greenwood Press, 1976), 292. Thomas P. Roche, Jr., *The Kindly Flame: A Study of the Third and Fourth Books of Spenser's* Faerie Queene (Princeton: Princeton Univ. Press, 1964), 32. Michael Murrin, *The Allegorical Epic: Essays in Its Rise and Decline* (Chicago: Univ. of Chicago Press, 1980), 144.

6. Those critics who note distinctions between Faeryland and places outside of it include the following.

Eden: John Upton, ed., *The Faerie Queene* (1758), cited in Edwin Greenlaw et al., eds., *The Works of Edmund Spenser: A Variorum Edition*, 10 vols. (Baltimore: Johns Hopkins Press, 1932–57), 1:312 (subsequently cited as *Variorum*); Isabel E. Rathborne, *The Meaning of Spenser's Fairyland* (New York: Columbia Univ. Press, 1937), 201; Isabel G. MacCaffrey, *Spenser's Allegory: The Anatomy of Imagination* (Princeton: Princeton Univ. Press, 1976), 209; Stephen A. Barney, *Allegories of History, Allegories of Love* (Hamden, CT: Archon Books, 1979), 108; Patricia A. Parker, *Inescapable Romance: Studies in the Poetics of a Mode* (Princeton: Princeton Univ. Press, 1979), 76.

Land of Mercilla, Ireland, and Western Europe: T.K. Dunseath, *Spenser's Allegory of Justice in Book Five of* The Faerie Queene (Princeton: Princeton Univ. Press, 1968), 207; Angus Fletcher, *The Prophetic Moment: An Essay on Spenser* (Chicago: Univ. of Chicago Press, 1971), 158; Andrew Fichter, *Poets Historical: Dynastic Epic in the Renaissance* (New Haven: Yale Univ. Press, 1982), 201.

Cleopolis: James Nohrnberg, *The Analogy of* The Faerie Queene (Princeton: Princeton Univ. Press, 1976), 207.

Wales: Ralph Church, ed., *The Faerie Queene* (1758–9), cited in *Variorum*, 3:215; Edwin Greenlaw, "Spenser's Fairy Mythology," *Studies in Philology* 15 (1918): 121; Charles Bowie Millican, *Spenser and the Table Round: A Study of the Contemporaneous Background for Spenser's Use of the Arthurian Legend* (Cambridge: Harvard Univ. Press, 1932), 146; Rathborne, 189, 201–3; Harry Berger, Jr., *The Allegorical Temper: Vision and*

Reality in Book II of Spenser's Faerie Queene (New Haven: Yale Univ. Press, 1957), 167; M. Pauline Parker, *The Allegory of* The Faerie Queene (Oxford: Clarendon Press, 1960), 11; MacCaffrey, 71; Ronald Arthur Horton, *The Unity of* The Faerie Queene (Athens, GA: Univ. of Georgia Press, 1978), 31; Anthea Hume, *Edmund Spenser: Protestant Poet* (Cambridge: Cambridge Univ. Press, 1984), 146–56.

7. Stephen Greenblatt, *Renaissance Self-Fashioning: From More to Shakespeare* (Chicago: Univ. of Chicago Press, 1980), 3. Greenblatt borrows the phrase "cultural artifact" from Clifford Geertz. New historicist and cultural materialist critics alike assume that, in Richard Helgerson's words, human "identity is a structure, a cultural construct" (*Forms of Nationhood: The Elizabethan Writing of England* [Chicago: Univ. of Chicago Press, 1992], 13). Compare Jonathan Dollimore, *Radical Tragedy: Religion, Ideology and Power in the Drama of Shakespeare and His Contemporaries* (Chicago: Univ. of Chicago Press, 1984), 17–9. And see Jean E. Howard, "The New Historicism in Renaissance Studies," *English Literary Renaissance* 16 (1986), who regards "the notion that man is a construct, not an essence" (23) as "the core of a truly new historical criticism" (20); and Edward Pechter, "The New Historicism and Its Discontents: Politicizing Renaissance Drama," *PMLA* 102 (1987), who provides a critique of the issue (300–2).

8. E.M.W. Tillyard, *The Elizabethan World Picture: A Study of the Idea of Order in the Age of Shakespeare, Donne and Milton* (1943; rpt. London: Chatto and Windus, 1973), passim.

9. Greenblatt, *Self-Fashioning*, 174. Compare Gary Waller, *English Poetry of the Sixteenth Century* (London: Longman, 1986), 206.

10. According to Greenblatt's theory of containment, Elizabethan culture, one step ahead of subversive forces, creates an alien other in order to destroy it; thus, Spenser creates Acrasia's Bower of Bliss for Guyon to destroy it in an act of sexual colonialism that reflects "the European response to the native cultures of the New World, the English colonial struggle in Ireland, and the Reformation attack on images" (*Self-Fashioning*, 179). Greenblatt duly quotes Freud (*Civilization and Its Discontents*, trans. James Strachey [New York: Norton, 1962], 51): "'Civilization behaves toward sexuality as a people or a stratum of its population does which has subjected another one to its exploitation'" (173).

11. Although cultural materialism, the British neo-Marxist manifestation of revisionist historicism, reserves some potential in its program for limited human agency within and even outside the structures of power, its own monolithic focus on class warfare as the defining force in history reduces textual meaning to politico-economic negotiations inevitably dominated by the oppressors. The producers of texts as well as the producers of criticism

remain, at best, pawns in the game of power, whispering resistance or dutifully reproducing sanctioned ideologies amid the din of master voices. No space exists for creative expression unmediated by the sources of power, no theoretical license for the relatively free play of meaning that *The Faerie Queene* often invites.

12. According to Greenblatt (*Self-Fashioning*, 192), "Spenser's art does not lead us to perceive ideology critically, but rather affirms the existence and inescapable moral power of ideology as that principle of truth toward which art forever yearns." Jonathan Goldberg's linguistic determinism leaves art doubly tainted, for art not only inevitably speaks a language given by ideology but also necessarily oversteps its legitimate bounds by speaking the unspeakable: "*The Faerie Queene* speaks the language of power, hedging itself round with disclaimers, denying the poet's voice in order to proclaim the truth, a truth that is not its own" since "the poet's words are at the sovereign's command" ("The Poet's Authority: Spenser, Jonson, and James VI and I," in *The Power of Forms in the English Renaissance*, ed. Stephen Greenblatt [Norman, OK: Pilgrim Books, 1982], 92, 81). Compare Goldberg, *Endlesse Worke*, 122–74. Richard Helgerson sees the poet participating in the cooptation of his fictional world: "The imagining of a 'second world' . . . has at its origin a negative response to the first world of our ordinary experience. But that response is typically enclosed, qualified, and conventionalized" in such a way that it reinforces "the authority of the governing order by placing its perfecting negation safely beyond reach" ("Inventing Noplace, or the Power of Negative Thinking," in *Power of Forms*, ed. Greenblatt, 104). Compare Greenblatt, *Self-Fashioning*, 190–2.

13. For general evaluations of recent historicist criticism, see, for example, Jonathan Goldberg, "The Politics of Renaissance Literature: A Review Essay," *ELH* 49 (1982): 514–42; Jean Howard, "New Historicism," 13–43; Louis A. Montrose, "Renaissance Literary Studies and the Subject of History," *English Literary Renaissance* 16 (1986): 5–12; Jean Howard and Marion O'Conner, eds., *Shakespeare Reproduced* (New York: Methuen, 1987); Pechter, "New Historicism," 292–303; H. Aram Vesser, ed., *The New Historicism* (New York: Routledge, 1989).

14. Alan Sinfield, "Power and Ideology: An Outline Theory and Sidney's *Arcadia*," *ELH* 52 (1985): 275. For cultural materialist commentary on new historicism, see Jonathan Dollimore, "Introduction: Shakespeare, Cultural Materialism and the New Historicism," in *Political Shakespeare: New Essays in Cultural Materialism*, ed. Dollimore and Sinfield (Ithaca: Cornell Univ. Press, 1985), 2–17; *Uses of History: Marxism, Postmodernism and the Renaissance*, ed. Francis Barker, Peter Hulme and Margaret Iversen (Manchester: Manchester Univ. Press, 1991).

15. Louis Adrian Montrose, "The Elizabethan Subject and the Spenserian Text," in *Literary Theory/Renaissance Texts*, ed. Patricia Parker and David Quint (Baltimore: Johns Hopkins Univ. Press, 1986), 331. Montrose continues: "Thus, Spenser's text may be said to constitute the identity of its Subject/Author in an interplay between the subject's gestures of subjection and the author's gestures of authority—in those paradoxical celebrations of power that, in making the poem serve the queen, make the queen serve the poem" (331–2). Concluding his article, Montrose gestures toward the critic's own agency: "In reflecting upon my own practice in the foregoing essay, I am aware of a strong stake, not in any illusion of individual autonomy but in the possibilities for limited and localized agency within the regime of power that at once sustains and constrains us" (333).

16. Helgerson, *Forms of Nationhood*, 12–3; see also 9, 24.

17. Stephen Greenblatt, "The Circulation of Social Energy," in *Shakespearean Negotiations: The Circulation of Social Energy in Renaissance England* (Berkeley: Univ. of California Press, 1988), 2. Qualifying his earlier pronouncements, Greenblatt states that "[e]ven those literary texts that sought most ardently to speak for monolithic power could be shown to be sites of institutional and ideological contestation" (3) and goes as far as suggesting that "the social energy encoded in certain works of art continues to generate the illusion of life for centuries" (7). In "Kindly Visions" (*New Yorker*, 11 October 1993, 112–20), a review of a book about *National Geographic*, Greenblatt all but apologizes for his earlier excesses (see 119–20). He has not yet, to my knowledge, applied these qualifications to his interpretation of *The Faerie Queene*.

18. See Helgerson, *Forms*, "The Land Speaks," 105–47; and Lawrence Manley, "From Matron to Monster: Tudor-Stuart London and the Languages of Urban Description," in *The Historical Renaissance: New Essays in Tudor and Stuart Literature and Culture*, ed. Heather Dubrow and Richard Strier (Chicago: Univ. of Chicago Press, 1988), 347–74.

19. The tendency of meaning in allegory to be ambiguous and therefore to proliferate in potentially dangerous ways motivates Spenser to write the Letter to Ralegh in the first place and might also be the reason Ralegh "command[s]" Spenser to write. See Goldberg, *Endlesse Worke*, 28; and Kenneth Gross, *Spenserian Poetics: Idolatry, Iconoclasm, and Magic* (Ithaca: Cornell Univ. Press, 1985), 17.

20. In the Letter to Ralegh, Spenser exploits the irony inherent in allegory's dual tendencies toward accessibility and concealment. (On this dual tendency, see Jacqueline T. Miller, *Poetic License: Authority and Authorship in Medieval and Renaissance Contexts* [New York: Oxford Univ. Press, 1986], 81–85, 195–99, nn. 16–29.) He presents a theory of allegorical composition in

which the superficial "showes" constituted in the "Allegoricall deuises" serve to make "discipline" accessible and therefore didactically potent by delighting and pleasing "commune sence"—the common audience that responds to ornament and to titillation of the senses. He also dresses his statements about his method in metaphors of darkness, disguise, and clouding that suggest hidden or esoteric meanings inaccessible to the audience he presumably seeks to attract in order to enlighten. A further irony might inhabit Spenser's strategy, for his condescending attitude toward his popular audience might flatter those grave gentlemen who disdain poetry while his metaphors of darkness might tempt them, and further flatter them, to consider themselves among the elite capable of revealing hidden meaning. Spenser does just this in his dedicatory sonnet to Burghley: in presenting his "ydle rimes" to the august lord, he argues that the "dim vele" of allegory, to which Burghley would presumably object, hides the "fairer parts" from "comune vew," flattering the "mighty Peres" (6.12.41) potential ability to weigh the "deeper sence" of the "rimes," in which case "[p]erhaps not vaine they may appeare" (*The Faerie Queene*, ed. Hamilton, 741).

In the Proem to Book 2, Spenser advertises yet another justification for his allegorical method, again making his expression of theory consistent with his audience, this time his whole audience, popular and elite alike. Spenser tells Elizabeth why he must "enfold / In covert vele" her presence in the poem: "That feeble eyes your glory may behold, / Which else could not endure those beames bright, / But would be dazled with exceeding light." If he did not "wrap" her "light" in "shadowes," his readers' "eyes" would be so "dazled" that they could not see to read (5). Instead of competing with or obscuring truth, allegory here participates in truth as the vehicle by which it is disclosed. In all, Spenser's public voice fits the theory to the occasion, and then the poet does whatever he wants in the poetry itself.

21. Gordon Teskey, "Allegory," in *The Spenser Encyclopedia*, ed. A.C. Hamilton et al. (Toronto: Univ. of Toronto Press, 1990), 17, 18.

22. Gross, *Spenserian Poetics*, 82; Parker, *Inescapable Romance*, 69, 54–113 passim; Teskey, "Irony, Allegory, and Metaphysical Decay," *PMLA* 109 (1994): 405. See Balachandra Rajan, "Closure," *Spenser Encyclopedia*, 169–70.

Chapter I
Epic and History

Concerned to assert the epic status of a poem dominated by the conventions of romance, Spenser situates Faeryland within an epic cosmos, anchors his narrative to history by constructing a political geography around Faeryland, and variously displays his poem's adherence to traditional epic conventions. He defends a predominately romance and allegorical poem by emphasizing its epic and heroic attributes, particularly its historical subject matter. At the same time, he sometimes invests his often defensive maneuvers with subtly ironic suggestions of alternate agendas and with covert gibes at unimaginative readers, neoclassical epic purists, and myopic Tudor propagandists.

In the first lines of the Proem to Book 1 of *The Faerie Queene*, Spenser declares his poem an epic, albeit his own kind—a "continued Allegory, or darke conceit. . . . coloured with an historicall fiction"—by imitating the lines that introduce Renaissance editions of the *Aeneid*; but he immediately qualifies, complicates, and supplements the reference to Virgil by imitating Ariosto's opening of the *Orlando Furioso*, itself an imitation of the *Aeneid*'s first lines. Spenser goes on, in epic wise: he invokes the aid of Clio, Calliope, or both in revealing the "antique rolles" that record the history of Arthur's search for "fairest *Tanaquill*," the Faery Queen Gloriana (2); he engages the powers of the classical deities by calling upon Cupid, the source of the "glorious fire" that inspires Arthur's quest, to put aside his "deadly Heban bow" and, along with Venus, "come to [his] ayde," bringing Mars the lover along as well (3); and he solicits Elizabeth, "Goddesse heauenly bright," to enable his "argument" by inspiring him "To thinke of that true glorious type of thine." Finally, Spenser requests that the queen "vouchsafe" to "heare" what he has to say (4). While suspending romance—in both senses of the word—amid his epic invocation, Spenser uses the Proem to assert epic authority by appealing for and, implicitly, appropriating epic inspiration—license to write epic.

Walter Ralegh, Gabriel Harvey,[1] and others among the poet's friends confirm Spenser's epic intention—indeed, his epic achievement—in their commendatory verses, in which they eulogize England's first epic poet by placing Spenser in the classic line: he is "this Bryttane *Orpheus*," the English counterpart to Homer and Petrarch, and, most significantly, England's own Virgil.[2] Spenser's friends also indicate the gravity of the epic poet's task. Harvey exclaims that "some sacred fury hath enricht [his friend's] braynes" and ruefully acknowledges Spenser's abandonment of the pastoral world:

> Thy louely Rosolinde seemes now forlorne,
> and all thy gentle flockes forgotten quight,
> Thy chaunged hart now holdes thy pypes in scorne,
> those prety pypes that did thy mates delight.

He sees the epic poet leaving his "trustie mates" among the shepherds and forsaking the security of the pastoral world to "chaunt heroique deedes" and "feast the humour of the Courtly traine" with his "pleasing style."[3] Since the epic poet's duty to tradition demands that he sing the glory of his nation, he must praise a national hero and picture the highest earthly perfection in his sovereign. Ralegh—who ought to know—advises that Spenser address the queen tactfully: "let her sole lookes deuine / Iudge if ought therein be amis, and mend it by her eine." W.I. suggests that just as Ulysses brought Achilles out of hiding, "the chaunce of warre to try," so Sidney convinced Spenser to undertake the most challenging poetic task: "To blaze [Elizabeth's] fame not fearing future harmes. . . . What though his taske exceed a humaine witt, / He is excus'd, sith *Sidney* thought it fitt." In the Commendatory Verses, Spenser's friends and fellow poets assert the epic status of *The Faerie Queene*, indicate the potentially hazardous political consequences that attend the epic poet's task, commend Spenser to the queen, and request that he be accorded the same "leaues of fame" as were bestowed upon Virgil and Petrarch.[4]

In the Letter to Ralegh, Spenser defends his poem against those who might question its epic status or misconstrue the allegory, emphasizing the historical foundation of his subject matter and outlining his grand allegorical design while demonstrating his acute awareness of the dangers and expectations implicit in his epic task. His comments, notably learned and conservative (though ultimately playful and ironic), characterize the poet's public voice, expressing his consciousness of his grave responsibility to portray truth for his age. In asserting the historical basis of his subject matter, Spenser takes a stand in the debate over the relative value of history and poetry as approaches to truth; in doing so, he manifests the dominant Renaissance attitude toward fictitious narrative, concisely described by William Nelson: "The great mass of Renaissance literary criticism . . . defended the proposition that though fiction was not the truth of history it was nevertheless truth in some other, more profound sense. Throughout this voluminous literature of apology, the reader senses a continuing and never fully resolved struggle against a stubborn conviction that true report was superior to any imitation of it, that despite the claims of invented narrative to moral, religious, or philosophical verity and despite the example of the great poems of antiquity, fiction remained no more than a counterfeit of reality, delightful perhaps and suitable for recreation but not for the mature attention of grown men."[5] While assessing the cultural obstacles confronting Spenser's professional laureate ambitions, Richard Helgerson acknowledges essentially the same point: "The lesson of poetry was . . . to stay away from poetry and from everything associated with it."[6] Nonetheless, poets and literary critics sought to vindicate what they considered the best and most worthwhile poetry—epic and tragic—by responding to the charges of untruth leveled against poetry in general. Their responses, as often replies to powerful cultural assumptions as to particular documents, defend the truth and value of epic and tragic poetry insofar as these kinds imitate history and serve an exemplary purpose equal to the unadorned examples of history.[7] Epic poets had to find the best means of imitating truth and the surest method of instructing their audiences. They found authoritative models in Homer, Virgil, and other classical epic poets, and discursive analysis of the issues confronting them in Aristotle's *Poetics* (Latin translation, 1498; printed Greek text, 1508) and in the vast commentary that flowed from it.

Out of the great body of sixteenth-century practical and theoretical criticism, Torquato Tasso's *Discourses on the Heroic Poem*,[8] written perhaps as early as 1565 and published in 1594, serves as a useful introduction to Spenser's moderate neoclassical stance on epic narrative in the Letter to Ralegh, however much of Ariosto there may be in *The Faerie Queene*. Tasso outlines "the conditions that a judicious poet should seek in his material . . . : the authority of history, the truth of religion, opportunity for invention, propriety in the era, and greatness in the events."[9] The epic poet must present a "narration of a memorable and possible human action" because "the most perfect poetry imitates things that are, were, or may be, such as the Trojan war, the wrath of Achilles, Aeneas's piety, the battles of the Trojans and Latins, and other things that either happened or might have happened." In a guarded qualification, Tasso admits that although the epic poet has "a perpetual obligation to preserve verisimilitude, . . . one same action can be marvelous and verisimilar" if the action is attributed to "God and his ministers."[10]

Tasso distinguishes four genres of poetry—heroic, tragic, comic, and lyric—and treats epic and romance not as distinct genres but, rather, as two kinds of heroic narrative. The epic kind, synonymous with "best poetry," is a unified, verisimilar narration of a single memorable action performed by a single hero out of history. The romance kind differs from the epic, according to Tasso and most other Italian Renaissance critics, in two ways: it has a multiple plot involving multiple heroes and is therefore ununified, or unified in a manner different from that prescribed by Aristotle; and it includes relatively more and more unrestrained fantastic imitation of marvelous events and therefore stretches the limits of verisimilitude.[11] The defenders of romance—those who support Ariosto in the literary quarrel begun in earnest by Fornari in 1549 and focused in practical criticism after the publication of the *Gerusalemme Liberata* in 1581 (unauthorized publication, 1575)—argue that both the multiple plot and the marvelous events have ancient precedents and add variety to the fiction, thus serving to delight and astonish the audience. They reason, like Sidney in his defense of poetry, that the variety and wonder of the invention draw readers to virtuous behavior by pleasing them. Tasso agrees that variety and wonder are important ingredients of any epic poem and that poetry instructs at least as successfully as history, but he insists that the greatest poetry must observe the norms of heroic epic—verisimilitude, historical subject matter, and unity of plot. Although Tasso's terminology conditionally legitimates romance form and matter, his pronounced bias, which intensifies neurotically as he ages, betrays his obvious preference for epic over romance.

The persistent, underlying assumption in Renaissance commentary on romance—that its relative fictionality makes it intrinsically inferior to epic—accounts for the value judgments of the neoclassical critics as well as for the apologetic tone of the defenders of romance. When literary critics chose to disagree with Aristotle by naming the highest poetry epic rather than tragic, they merely asserted a preference for narrative over dramatic literature; tragedy remained the preferred drama and epic the preferred narrative. Making the *Poetics* consistent with the new arrangement was simple, since the crucial Aristotelian doctrine concerning tragedy could be transferred to epic. Aristotle does this himself when he describes the epic as an extended tragedy or series of tragedies, emphasizing the probability of the tragic action and suggesting historical events as the best subjects for tragedy.[12] In turn, Renaissance critics demanded verisimilitude and historical subject matter in epic poetry.[13] And the value judgment is built in: tragedy and epic are the best, truest, and most valuable poetry because they present the greatest human actions within the world of history; comedy concerns common or foolish persons and actions, and romance often lacks a firm setting in the real world. Epic is founded on fact and romance on fiction, and since fact possesses greater authority than fiction, epic is the higher form.

Essentially the same judgment of value persists in the work of W.P. Ker, E.M.W. Tillyard, Maurice Bowra, Albert Cook, Thomas Greene, and most other modern writers on the epic.[14] In both Renaissance and modern criticism this value judgment leads logically to another: the term *epic* becomes an expression of appreciation, the name for those long narratives the critic most admires; other narratives become little more than failed epics, and the phrase "fully successful romance" becomes either a misnomer or an oxymoron. This state of critical affairs has been the catalyst for generations of apologists for Spenser's apparently romance matter and manner.

Spenser's Letter to Ralegh inherits the apologetic tone of the defenders of the new poetry in Italy, those who sought epic status for Dante and Ariosto or defended the equal validity of romance and epic narrative; at the same time, it absorbs the neoclassical criticism of Italy and France and demonstrates Spenser's expertise in the theory and methods of Renaissance historiography.[15] The Letter—a politico-literary act of damage control, cultural criticism, and rhetorical play—re-presents *The Faerie Queene* in accord with the expectations of its various audiences and in response to the conditions of Elizabethan literary production. On its surface, the Letter's public address advertises the poem's embrace of unadorned history and moral philosophy, treating fiction and allegory as the suspect but necessary means of achieving the national poet's didactic purpose; at the same time, other authorial voices lurk in the text, addressing other audiences, representing the poem in other ways, and exploiting the resources of language play afforded by the Letter's highly charged and potentially ambiguous terminology and examples.

In his public voice, Spenser upholds a conservative—condescending, skeptical, and relatively disparaging—attitude toward fiction and allegory that bears pointed contrast to Philip Sidney's pronouncements in the *Defence of Poesie*.[16] Spenser says that he has "coloured" his "continued Allegory" with "an historicall fiction" to make it "most plausible and pleasing"; history supplies the plausibility and fiction supplies the pleasure. He introduces "an historicall *fiction*" (italics added) because "the most part of men delight to read" a fictionalized account of history, "rather for variety of matter, then for profite of the ensample." That is, he appears to concede, fiction amounts to mere ornamentation since the "ensample" inheres in the historical record of events; fiction may be more "pleasing" to the majority of readers than unadorned history, but both serve the didactic purpose. Unlike Sidney, who celebrates the poet's fictional examples and challenges the exemplary usefulness of the historian's questionable facts,[17] Spenser, ostensibly, exhibits no preference for fiction and condescends to the poet's method out of necessity.

Likewise, Spenser's discussion of his allegorical method betrays a bias toward the austere learning of philosophers:

> To some I know this Methode will seem displeasaunt, which had rather haue good discipline deliuered plainly in way of precepts, or sermoned at large, as they vse, then thus clowdily enwrapped in Allegoricall deuises. But such, me seeme, should be satisfide with the vse of these dayes, seeing all things accounted by their showes, and nothing esteemed of, that is not delightful and pleasing to commune sence. For this cause is Xenophon preferred before Plato, for that the one in the exquisite depth of his iudgement, formed a Commune welth such as it should be, but the other in the person of Cyrus and the Persians fashioned a gouernement such as might best be: So much more profitable and gratious is doctrine by ensample, then by rule. So have I laboured to doe in the person of Arthure.

Just as fiction ornaments the bare facts of history, so allegory embellishes the stern precepts of philosophy. Spenser appears to be in essential agreement with Sidney, who argues that the poet uses fiction to enhance important but otherwise dry subject matter—history and philosophy—"even as the child is often brought to take most wholesome things by hiding them in such other as have a pleasant taste."[18] But Spenser's tone and emphasis diverge considerably from Sidney's. Sidney disparages the "thorny arguments" of the philosopher, "so hard of utterance and so misty to be conceived," and exposes the limited usefulness of the historian's facts. In turn, he celebrates the creative potential of the poet, who joins precept and example in a "speaking picture" that reveals not merely "what is" but rather "what should be": "he yieldeth to the powers of the mind an image of that whereof the philosopher bestoweth but a wordish description, which doth neither strike, pierce, nor possess the sight of the soul so much as that other doth."[19] Conversely, Spenser sees the philosopher Plato, not the poet

Xenophon, revealing what "should be" and suggests that allegory obscures or "clowd[s]" the "precepts" that are "deliuered plainly" by the philosopher.

Spenser assumes a relatively patronizing attitude toward the poet's use of fiction and allegory, comparing his "Allegoricall deuises" to mere "showes" that are "delightfull and pleasing to commune sence." He speaks the words of paternal authority, chiding those who require the enticement of fiction or allegory—Sidney's "medicine of cherries"[20]—to inspire moral behavior and draw them toward virtuous civic duty. But since, as Spenser admits, such is "the vse of these dayes," and since, as epic poet, he must attract a national audience, he concedes that allegorical "ensamples" provide a "more profitable and gratious" manner of instruction than the more straightforward doctrine "by rule."[21] Nonetheless, he insists that the allegory is merely the pleasing surface of a national epic built upon the firm foundation of unadorned history and ethical philosophy. This voice, which addresses those who would not hesitate to name more profitable activities than either reading or writing poetry, is at least relatively distinct from the voice of the poet whose *Faerie Queene* celebrates without apology the beauty and power of allegorical narrative in a fictional setting. This is not, however, to suggest flippancy or lack of resolve on Spenser's part concerning his desire to write epic and to portray history in his poem; rather, the irony implicit in his sometimes reactionary public voice in the Letter serves to call into question uncritical attitudes toward history and simplistic distinctions between fact and fiction.

Spenser makes his comments on subject matter roughly analogous to those on allegorical method, and he plays on history in some of the same ways he plays on allegorical devices. He says he "chose" to focus his "historicall fiction" on "the historye of king Arthure, as most fitte for the excellency of his person, being made famous by many mens former workes, and also furthest from the daunger of enuy, and suspition of present time." As a renowned, noble, and exemplary national hero who lived far enough in the past to be, apparently, immune to "suspition of present time," Arthur embodies the criteria that define the traditional epic hero. Moreover, his story supplies the single action demanded by classical precedent, and his virtue—"magnificence"—allows theoretical unity of plot by representing the sum of the other heroes' virtues. Spenser's matter of Arthur, with its source in sixth-century Britain and its culmination in sixteenth-century/prophetic Cleopolis, illustrates "the wel-head of the History," by which "the whole intention of the conceit" may be understood.

With a tempting dose of ambiguity juxtaposed to the serious considerations of a thoughtful antiquary historian about the relation of historical inquiry to myth, fable, legend, and chronicle, Spenser enters boldly into the controversy surrounding the Arthurian question. The dizzying array of literary critical and historiographical issues condensed into Spenser's exposition of his subject provides a fairly exhaustive inventory of the poet's responses to some of the major intellectual currents of his time, which might most simply be stated as an analogous series of familiar Renaissance debates between fact and fiction, history and poetry, and epic and romance. The European Renaissance, much less its English component, holds no monopoly on the basic intellectual issues at the root of these analogous pairs, but late sixteenth- and early seventeenth-century experimentation and discussion involving the forms and concepts implied by these words were centrally important in producing modern historical discourse and fictional narrative.

In the portions of the Letter dealing with the Arthurian subject matter, Spenser's innovative participation in signal issues of his day includes a satisfactory display of the official view, some ironic play, and, most significantly, fascinating revisionist suggestions about the relation of poetry to history. To the Tudor leadership and its many chauvinistic partisans, who, finding in the Arthurian material—particularly the myth of Arthur's return—a valuable propagandistic tool, sought to preserve the unquestioned authority of Geoffrey of Monmouth's account, Spenser offers a straight "historye of king Arthure" coupled with a narrative invention that brings Arthur into direct coordination (not to say intimate contact) with Elizabeth as Faery Queen.[22] In *The Faerie Queene* itself, Spenser presents chronicle accounts which, at least superficially, ratify Tudor legend. At the same time, Spenser plays on the alternate connotation of the word *history*, fashioning the Arthurian material as mere story or fable, for the "historye" turns out to be an entirely fabulous contrivance, the story of Arthur "before he was king," which even the most reactionary Tudor propagandists would be forced to scoff at as romance fluff. As for the "former workes" by which Arthur had been "made famous," there is no sure means of knowing what Spenser may have had in mind, but he is likely to be once again playing on both words and contemporary options. In this case, *famous* might as easily mean controversial or even notorious as renowned; and *workes* could refer as readily to Geoffrey of Monmouth's *Historia* and the voluminous romance material that flowed in part from it, to Polydore Virgil's scandalous debunking of the myth of Arthur in his *Anglica Historia* (1534) and John Leland's dutifully reactionary *Assertio* (1544), or, more generally, to all the polemical works that produced what Edwin Greenlaw named the "sixteenth century battle of the books."[23] Spenser was, at least in his public persona, probably one with William Camden in being "content to survey the prospect,"[24] though even such a mildly undogmatic stance could have appeared dangerous in some quarters; as Charles Bowie Millican observes after quoting an anonymous attack on Polydore Virgil concluding with the exhortation that the debunker be hanged, "when Ponsonby was printing *The Faerie Queene*, the Arthurian wing of the Ancients was in triumph over the Moderns, and without sweetness and light."[25] Whatever Spenser refers to as the source of Arthur's fame, he selects controversial Arthurian subject matter for his epic; rather than choosing legendary material from the distant past that was indeed "furthest from the daunger of enuy, and suspition of present time," as epic poets since Virgil had been wont to do, Spenser sets himself squarely in the heat of political and intellectual debate. In portraying the youthful Arthur, Spenser conceives an epic while embracing the radical fringe of romance writing, in effect suspending judgment on the historical Arthur while revaluating the whole situation in the light of a new generic classification, the allegorical historical fiction. Moreover, by consciously avoiding the terms *epic*, *heroic*, and *romance*, Spenser effectively thwarts criticism based on generic expectations and thereby preserves some measure of creative freedom.

Spenser's experimentation with genre and his sophisticated rethinking of the issues surrounding the Arthurian legends are intimately related to his active role in what, following F. Smith Fussner's groundbreaking work, has come to be known as the English "historical revolution," the development of modern approaches to historical inquiry that began to accelerate during the last two decades of the sixteenth century, in spite of the stultifying effects of Tudor propaganda.[26] One way of assessing Spenser's historiographical perspective in the Letter is to call once again on Sidney in the *Defence* as a magisterial and eminently serviceable foil. When Sidney sets the poet's didactic value up against the historian's, he presents two versions of historical methodology that show him to be fully conversant with the state of historiography in his time. He depicts a whimsically sophisticated portrait of the humanist historian, who advertises an exemplar theory of history and beats the moralist philosopher at his own game by manipulating his "mouse-eaten records, authorizing himself (for the most part) upon other histories, whose greatest authorities are built upon the notable foundation of hearsay." This historian "denieth, in great chafe, that any man for teaching of virtue, and virtuous actions is comparable to him." Sidney also presents a telling description of the new scientific or empirical historian, who, "being captived to the truth of a foolish world" and "wanting the precept, is so tied, not to what should be but to what is, to the particular truth of things and not to the general reason of things, that his example draweth no necessary consequence, and therefore a less fruitful doctrine."[27] The former fulfills his duty as teacher of virtue only by playing the poet's part while the latter abandons his didactic responsibility in the face of hard facts.

Writing sometime before 1580, Sidney exposes some very real limitations in contemporary historiography, limitations that become even more pronounced when, as with Spenser, political issues replace moral didacticism, when Arthur replaces ethics in Sidney's portraits. In that case, we have either time-serving patriots whose nationalist frenzy or envious fear drives them to sacrifice their status as legitimate historians to preserve the mythical Arthur; or we have a few empiricist chroniclers willing to breast the tide of political pressure by presenting a historical Arthur, a minor sixth- or seventh-century Briton or Saxon chieftain whose story gives no indication of the massive cultural significance of this historical nobody. Spenser brings Arthur into his revisionist literary historiography by employing the perspective of a poet historical who merges and supplements Sidney's pair of historians: by combining the methods of the humanist and the empiricist with those of the antiquary, Spenser constructs cultural history.

As an innovative participant in the new history, Spenser respects the authority of verifiable sources; Arthur B. Ferguson claims that when Spenser wrote *A View of the Present State of Ireland*, he proceeded "with an empirical treatment of evidence which bore developmental, even progressivist implications."[28] Long before Spenser composed *A View*, this methodology helped to shape his conception of *The Faerie Queene*'s Arthur as a legendary component of political history. Although Spenser probably did not "take the Arthurian legends at their face value,"[29] he realized that questioning Arthur's historicity did not cancel his value as a cultural exemplum. However, this is only the initial step toward a revised historiography that truly, so to speak, puts Arthur in his place; to broadly based research and critical assessment of data must be added some room for educated guesswork that could yield a creative yet empirically grounded reconstruction of the past. This methodology both inspired and was inspired by the beginnings of a recognition by Spenser and some of his fellow antiquaries that the frontier between history and myth was not so clearly defined as even the most enlightened chroniclers assumed, and that historical inquiry could yield other kinds of fruits besides narratives of political events. In the course of investigating, collecting, and recording all manner of cultural texts, these sixteenth-century antiquary historians were beginning to explore and interpret "that broad and ill-defined area of historical experience which stretched beyond *res gestae*"; in doing so, they exposed the domain of cultural myth and stumbled upon the theory of cultural change that became the foundation of modern historical thought.[30] According to Ferguson, Francis Bacon put into historiographical practice what Spenser and his fellow antiquaries discovered: "he was able to recognize more clearly than any Englishman had done hitherto the significance of myths in the history of culture and the ability of the historical imagination, the faculty most nearly akin to Spenser's concept of the 'poet historical,' to penetrate that cloudy region."[31]

Spenser saw that the myth of Arthur was of far greater significance to the history of England than random political facts about a minor figure out of ancient history, for he understood that the unrealized potential of history often takes the form of cultural myths which, in turn, motivate historical events.[32] In Spenser's "historye of king Arthur," empiricist historiography, cultural mythology, and poetic inspiration intersect and define one another in a maze of coordinated conflicts. Spenser portrays in the Letter an invented youthful Arthur who, having been "rauished" "in a dream or vision" by the "excellent beauty" of "the Faery Queen," wanders Faeryland in search of her (1.9.12–15), never succeeding Uther to the throne of sixth-century Britain. Instead, at the crucial moment (2.10.68), Spenser excises the historical Arthur from his poem and from chronicle history; the historical Arthur ceases to exist except as an inference born of an absence in the minds of readers whose conscious or unconscious cognizance of cultural myth instinctively mends the gap that stands open at the end of *Briton moniments*. Spenser never closes this narrow but crucial breach in Tudor genealogy between Uther and Cador's son Constantius (3.3.27–9); Arthur's reign and, strictly speaking, everything that goes with it, disappears from British political history. And the time-honored observation that Artegall replaces Arthur in *The Faerie Queene*'s chronicles simply cannot explain away either the Arthurian vacancy or Spenser's audacity in appropriating the power to manipulate history. Spenser creates an ellipsis in the British succession, obfuscates chronicle history by leaving Artegall's son nameless, and presumptuously supplies the Tudors with a newly fabricated (or fashioned) royal genealogy descending from the Cornish Artegall's "Image dead," the son of two pseudo-historical inventions (3.3.29).

Spenser, Ralegh, and, yes, Burghley, knew that these machinations illustrate perfectly why and how poets can be dangerous and useless; and they all probably also knew that the dangerous or fearful can be pacified by and absorbed into ideological myth, which is exactly what Spenser does in his poem. For despite his bold and perhaps ironic assertion of history-making potential, his poem serves the historical Arthur whose very absence engenders the almost sovereign power of myth as cultural determinant. Spenser's "historye of king Arthur" is at once a unifying narrative invention, an epic political quest set in the distant past, a myth of national destiny embodying the prophetic potential of history, and an allegorical investigation of ethical action. According to Spenser's long-range plans for his poem,

Arthur will be initiating Tudor apocalypse by serving and marrying Gloriana while Artegall (like Aeneas) is being "Too rathe cut off by practise criminall / Of secret foes" in sixth-century Britain, leaving his son to wrest the crown from Constantius, Artegall's (and Arthur's?) nephew (3.3.28–9). Perhaps Spenser's Arthur was inspired by patriotic fervor, perhaps by objective historicist analysis, but probably by some of each in combination with the mind of a genius who harbors a touch of ironic humor and skepticism.

Spenser uses the Letter to emphasize his poem's historical subject matter and to outline a plot structure consistent with the norms of epic. Yet he hardly mentions the setting in which his epic narrative unfolds, except to note an allegorical relationship between Faeryland and Elizabethan England: "In that Faery Queene I meane glory in my generall intention, but in my particular I conceiue the most excellent and glorious person of our soueraine the Queene, and her kingdome in Faery land"; that is, the allegorical relationship between Elizabeth and the Faery Queen mirrors that between England and Faeryland.[33] Spenser may avoid further discussion for very good reasons: first, locations within Faeryland have, at best, fluid and indistinct relationships to actual time and space; and, second, no other epic poet in the classic line sets the main action in an imaginary world. Homer, Virgil, Ariosto, and Tasso set most of their poems' action in identifiable geographical locales; epic poets include in their poems journeys to mythical, invented, and unknown worlds, but none sets the majority of the action in one of these places. Epic actions occur in the known world of political history.

In the Proem to Book 2, Spenser confronts the charges that might be leveled against an epic whose primary setting is a place called Faeryland:

> Right well I wote most mighty Soueraine,
> That all this famous antique history,
> Of some th'aboundance of an idle braine
> Will iudged be, and painted forgery,
> Rather then matter of iust memory,
> Sith none, that breatheth liuing aire, does know,
> Where is that happy land of Faery,
> Which I so much do vaunt, yet no where show,
> But vouch antiquities, which no body can know.
>
> (2.Proem.1)

Spenser views his poem as susceptible to rebuke not because of its multiple plot, its fantastic imitations, or its allegorical mode, but simply because no one knows the location of Faeryland. According to the logic Spenser chooses to pursue, Faeryland's unidentifiable location suggests its nonexistence, which, in turn, makes its narrative unverifiable and therefore vulnerable to attack by the detractors of poetry and the critics of romance narrative. *The Faerie Queene*—vain product of an "idle braine"—is idle entertainment for dangerously idle minds and, worse, "painted forgery," a falsehood that seeks to deceive, an ornamented lie, not an accurate record of verifiable events, not the unadorned truth of history, not "matter of iust memory." Spenser confronts the "simple challenge" that faces any Renaissance defender of poetry: "why any mature and virtuous person should write or read fiction, that is, an account of things that never occurred."[34]

While confessing that Faeryland seems no more than an invented supposition whose existence cannot be verified, Spenser attempts to prove its existence by analogy:

> But let that man with better sence aduize,
> That of the world least part to vs is red:
> And dayly how through hardy enterprize,
> Many great Regions are discouered,
> Which to late age were neuer mentioned.
> Who euer heard of th'Indian *Peru*?
> Or who in venturous vessell measured
> The *Amazons* huge riuer now found trew?
> Or fruitfullest *Virginia* who did euer vew?
>
> Yet all these were, when no man did them know;
> Yet haue from wisest ages hidden beene:
> And later times things more vnknowne shall show.
> Why then should witlesse man so much misweene
> That nothing is, but that which he hath seene?
> What if within the Moones faire shining spheare?
> What if in euery other starre vnseene
> Of other worldes he happily should heare?
> He wonder would much more: yet such to some appeare.
>
> (2.Proem.2–3)

Spenser argues that Faeryland exists in the same way that undiscovered earthly and heavenly regions exist, and he implies that one might, "through hardy enterprize," in fact discover Faeryland and other "hidden," "vnknowne," and "vnseene" realms. Assuming that his readers demand literal justification for his imagined world, Spenser gives them proof, and William Nelson points out the joke: "Fairyland exists because it has not yet been discovered. The logical absurdity should at least warrant a smile."[35]

Clearly, Faeryland and other "vnseene" realms—which "to some appeare"—exist not in the physical world but in the imagination, and "witlesse man" errs in thinking "That nothing is, but that which he hath seene," a fact that ought to be apparent to a Christian audience.

Spenser goes on to provide more specific instructions to those who remain unconvinced of Faeryland's reality:

> Of Faerie lond yet if he more inquire,
> By certaine signes here set in sundry place
> He may it find; ne let him then admire,
> But yield his sence to be too blunt and bace,
> That no'te without an hound fine footing trace.
> And thou, O fairest Princesse vnder sky,
> In this faire mirrhour maist behold thy face,
> And thine owne realmes in lond of Faery,
> And in this antique Image thy great auncestry.
>
> (2.Proem.4)

Spenser assures his audience that Faeryland may be found out by careful reading, but he warns that no hound is capable of following the "fine footing" that marks the way. Like explorers searching for new lands, though not in ordinary ships, readers must journey toward Faeryland on the "venturous vessell" of the imagination. When they get there, they will find a "mirrhour" and an "Image," allegorical entities different from but no less real than the actual entities they sought. In fact, the actual entity mirrored and shadowed in the allegory turns out to be so gloriously and dazzlingly real that it may be perceived only allegorically:

> The which O pardon me thus to enfold
> In couert vele, and wrap in shadowes light,
> That feeble eyes your glory may behold,
> Which else could not endure those beames bright,
> But would be dazled with exceeding light.
>
> (2.Proem.5)

In the Proem to Book 2, Faeryland begins as a nonentity and ends as transcendently real.

Spenser's logical procedure in the Proem to Book 2 resembles that of the Letter to Ralegh. In both, he anticipates attacks on his poem and meets them with apparently straightforward and conventional defenses that turn out to be ironic and sophisticated means of authorizing the integrity and efficacy of the narrative inventions for which he began by apologizing. Spenser plays with the naive notion of fiction as falsehood and exposes its obvious limitations, but such play does not dampen his resolve to create a credible world to house his combined epic and romance design. Aware of the revaluations of epic occasioned by the quarrel over Ariosto and Tasso, of the complex critical debates over the best means of achieving verisimilitude in fiction, and of the vast resources latent in his native medieval inheritance, Spenser invests his imaginative potency in creating a largely allegorical setting for his poem that is both verisimilar and historical. He creates the unique and multiform universe of *The Faerie Queene*.

Notes
Chapter I

1. In his commentary on "Januarye" in *The Shepheardes Calender*, E.K. provides the connection between Harvey and Hobbinol: "Hobbinol) is a fained country name, whereby, it being so commune and usuall, seemeth to be hidden the person of some his very speciall and most familiar freend, whom he entirely and extraordinarily beloved, as peradventure shall be more largely declared hereafter." Quoted from *The Yale Edition of the Shorter Poems of Edmund Spenser*, ed. William Oram et al. (New Haven: Yale Univ. Press, 1989), 33. This "freend," as he is portrayed in the *Calendar*, is probably a combination of references to Sidney, to whom "Immerito" (Spenser) dedicates his poem, and to Harvey, to whom E.K. addresses his dedicatory epistle. It is obviously not Sidney who writes the commendatory verse to *The Faerie Queene* in 1590 (having been dead for four years); the poem is clearly Harvey's, especially since it addresses the poet more familiarly than any of the others.

My text for the "Commendatory Verses" is *The Faerie Queene*, ed. A.C. Hamilton (London: Longman, 1977), 739–40.

2. R.S. cites Orpheus; H.B. compares Spenser's achievement to Virgil's. Ralegh (W.R.) writes that in a vision he "saw the graue, where *Laura* lay," then "All suddenly I saw the Faery Queene: / At whose approch the soule of *Petrarke* wept" (1, 6–7). The Graces move away from Laura and toward the Faery Queen:

For they this Queene attended, in whosc steed
Obliuion laid him downe on *Lauras* herse:
Hereat the hardest stones were seene to bleed,
And grones of buried ghostes the heauens did perse.
  Where *Homers* spright did tremble all for griefe,
  And curst th'accesse of that celestiall theife.

(9–14)

3. Hobynoll, "To the learned Shepheard," 7–10, 24.

4. W.R., "The prayse of meaner wits this worke like profit brings," 5–6; W.I., "When stout *Achilles* heard of *Helens* rape," 6, 16, 23–4; H.B., "Graue Muses march in triumph and with prayses," 8.

5. Nelson, *Fact and Fiction: The Dilemma of the Renaissance Storyteller* (Cambridge: Harvard Univ. Press, 1973), 8–9.

My brief comments on Renaissance literary criticism as it relates to Spenser's Letter to Ralegh are the product of readings in several sources other than the literary critical works themselves. For a comprehensive introduction to the major critical issues, I am indebted to J.E. Spingarn, *A History of Literary Criticism in the Renaissance* (1899; rpt. New York: Columbia Univ. Press, 1920). I found detailed commentary on most of what I needed to know about Italian Renaissance criticism in Bernard Weinberg's *A History of Literary Criticism in the Italian Renaissance*, 2 vols. (Chicago: Univ. of Chicago Press, 1961) and in Baxter Hathaway's *The Age of Criticism: The Late Renaissance in Italy* (Ithaca, NY: Cornell Univ. Press, 1962). Two shorter studies have been especially helpful: Nelson (cited above) focuses on the literary manifestations of the popular tendency to regard fiction as lies; Baxter Hathaway, *Marvels and Commonplaces: Renaissance Literary Criticism* (New York: Random House, 1968), focuses on "the conflict between the realistic and the marvelous" (viii). Nelson and Hathaway explore the two areas with which I am most concerned: the relation of history and verisimilitude to the Renaissance epic and to *The Faerie Queene* in particular. My main source for dates and details concerning Italian criticism is Weinberg. On the literary critical debate over *Orlando Furioso*, see Daniel Javitch, *Proclaiming a Classic: The Canonization of* Orlando Furioso (Princeton: Princeton Univ. Press, 1991).

6. Richard Helgerson, *Self-Crowned Laureates: Spenser, Jonson, Milton, and the Literary System* (Berkeley: Univ. of California Press, 1983), 64.

7. For a concise review of "the exemplar theory of history" see George F. Nadel, "Philosophy of History before Historicism," *History and Theory* 3 (1964): 291–315.

8. My text for Tasso's *Discorsi del Poema Eroico* is the translation by Mariella Cavalchini and Irene Samuel, *Discourses on the Heroic Poem* (Oxford: Clarendon Press, 1973).

9. Tasso, *Discourses*, 54. Tasso's "conditions that a judicious poet [i.e. epic poet] should seek" anticipate very closely E.M.W. Tillyard's general definition of epic in his comprehensive *The English Epic and its Background*, 5–13. According to Tillyard, the epic poem must be of "high quality" and its subject matter of "high seriousness"; it must be broad in its scope and controlled by a "structural ideal" and by the conscious will of the poet; and it must "express the feelings of a large group of people living in or near [the poet's] own time" by professing "faith in the system of beliefs or way of life it bears witness to."

10. Tasso, *Discourses*, 14, 30, 38.

11. Tasso, *Discourses*, 71–2. The word *genre* translates the Italian *spezie*.

12. My text for the *Poetics* is S. H. Butcher's translation in *Aristotle's Theory of Poetry and Fine Art*, 4th ed. (New York: Dover, 1955); rpt. in Hazard Adams, ed., *Critical Theory Since Plato* (New York: Harcourt, Brace, Jovanovich, 1971), 48–66. For Aristotle's comments on epic as a series of tragedies see ch. 24 (63). Aristotle argues that "it is not the function of the poet to relate what has happened, but what may happen." However, he notes that "tragedians still keep to real names, the reason being that what is possible is credible: What has not happened we do not at once feel sure to be possible" (ch. 9, 54).

E.M.W. Tillyard's thesis in *Shakespeare's History Plays* (London: Macmillan, 1944) is that Shakespeare writes what must be considered a dramatic epic in the cycle of eight plays dealing with English history from the reign of Richard II to the Battle of Bosworth (see especially 241–4, 262–3, 298–304). In *The English Epic* Tillyard asserts that "Shakespeare's historical sequences are the nearest existing approach to an Elizabethan epic" (14), primarily because they are "the greatest rendering of an English political theme in English" (65).

13. As Tillyard (*English Epic*) observes, there is a distinct Renaissance tendency, especially in England, "not to draw any clear line between the two narrative forms of epic and history" (203). Tillyard sees Lydgate in *The Fall of Princes* bringing the Renaissance epic theme to England because he writes exemplary history with the intention of instructing those who control political power (202). Likewise, Sidney's "new" *Arcadia* achieves "epic dignity" because it is "relatively more martial and political and less erotic than the old" (298), and Daniel's *Civil Wars* and even Drayton's *Polyolbion* were considered in their day both histories and heroic epic poems (336).

14. W.P. Ker, *Epic and Romance* (1896; rpt. New York: Dover, 1957); E.M.W. Tillyard, *English Epic*; Maurice Bowra, *From Virgil to Milton* (London: Macmillan, 1948); Albert Cook, *The Classic Line* (Bloomington, IL: Indiana Univ. Press, 1966); Thomas Greene, *The Descent From Heaven* (New Haven: Yale Univ. Press, 1963). Compare D.M. Hill, "Romance as Epic," *English Studies* 44 (1963): 95–107, who responds to Ker; Fichter, *Poets Historical* (1982), who views epic and romance in the Renaissance as two aspects of the Christian dynastic epic (see especially 17, 70–5, 85–90, 127–8, 156, 205–6); Helgerson, *Forms* (1992), who provides a new political and historicist reading of *The Faerie Queene* as a "Gothic" poem (see 23, 40–59); and Colin Burrow, *Epic Romance: Homer to Milton* (Oxford: Clarendon Press, 1993), who presents an original thesis that replaces traditional distinctions between epic and romance with a unified definition based on the theme of *pietas* (see 1–4, 120–7).

Tillyard, *English Epic*, avoids for the most part value judgments based on deviations from the heroic subject matter: "It was through the conviction of Dante's being as true an epic poet as Virgil that I abandoned any notion of using the heroic subject as a criterion. Finding the *Aeneid* closer in essentials to the *Divine Comedy* than to the *Argonautica* or *Gondibert*, I had to seek a definition of the epic other than the old heroic one" (5). Tillyard's approach allows him to include as English epics *Piers Plowman* and the *Arcadia* as well as *The Faerie Queene* and to note the native medieval influences on English epic, especially the allegory of the pilgrimage (see 134–78). At the same time, Tillyard's discussion of Elizabethan epic focuses on the exemplary historical subject matter that was demanded by that age (251–61). Thus, Tillyard is able to see Spenser consciously merging the medieval and Renaissance epics (262–93).

15. On the "new" historiography in Renaissance England, see F. Smith Fussner, *The Historical Revolution: English Historical Writing and Thought 1580–1640* (New York: Columbia Univ. Press, 1962); F.J. Levy, *Tudor Historical Thought* (San Marino, CA: Huntington Library, 1967); F. Smith Fussner, *Tudor History and the Historians* (New York: Basic Books, 1970); Arthur B. Ferguson, *Clio Unbound: Perception of the Social and Cultural Past in Renaissance England* (Durham, NC: Duke Univ. Press, 1979); D.R. Woolf, *The Idea of History in Early Stuart England: Erudition, Ideology, and "The Light of Truth" from the Accession of James I to the Civil War* (Toronto: Univ. of Toronto Press, 1990), 3–44. For a broader view of Renaissance historiography, see Denys Hays, *Annalists and Historians: Western Historiography from the Eighth to the Eighteenth Centuries* (London: Methuen, 1977), 87–168, and H. Butterfield, *The Statecraft of Machiavelli* (New York: Macmillan, 1956), 59–86 ("The 'Rise of the Inductive Method'").

16. My text for Sidney's *Defence* is from *Miscellaneous Prose of Sir Philip Sidney*, ed. Katherine Duncan-Jones and Jan Van Dorsten (Oxford: Clarendon Press, 1973), 73–121; see textual notes, 65–70.

17. Sidney, *Defence*, 83–4.

18. Sidney, *Defence*, 92.

19. Sidney, *Defence*, 83–5.

20. Sidney, *Defence*, 93.

21. Spenser states that Xenophon's "ensample" is "more profitable and gratious" than Plato's "doctrine . . . by rule." If Sidney had said this, which in effect he does (see *Defence*, 79, 86, 88), we would assume that he meant to praise the poet Xenophon over the philosopher Plato. But Spenser is subtly ironic. Note the condescending references to his "Allegoricall deuises" leading up to his mention of Xenophon. Spenser seeks justification for his clouding of plain precepts in "the vse of these dayes, seeing all things accounted by their showes, and nothing esteemed of, that is not delightfull and pleasing to commune sence. For this cause is Xenophon preferred before Plato." His avowed preference seems obvious enough. The words "profitable and gratious" refer, respectively, to "pleasing" and "delightful," not the kinds of words with which the epic poet would describe his poem. See entries under these words in *OED*; connotations of *profitable* involving monetary gain and of *gracious* involving favorable appearance provide an ironic context for Spenser's ambiguous use of the words.

22. For reviews of the Arthurian question in Elizabethan England, see Edwin Greenlaw, *Studies in Spenser's Historical Allegory* (Baltimore: Johns Hopkins Press, 1932), 1–58; and Charles Bowie Millican, *Spenser and the Table Round*, passim.

23. See Millican, 159, nn. 58–60. Millican (25) quotes Edwin Greenlaw from the *Program* of the 44th meeting of the Modern Language Association (1927), 4.

24. Millican, 90. See William Camden, *Britannia*, trans. Richard Gough (1806; rpt. Hildesheim: Georg-Olms Verlag, 1974), 1: lii–liii, 7.

25. Millican, 97.

26. Fussner, *Historical Revolution*. See note 15 above. Compare J.G.A. Pocock, "The Sense of History in Renaissance England," in *William Shakespeare: His World, His Work, His Influence*, ed. John F. Andrews, vol. 1, *His World* (New York: Scribners, 1985), 143–57. Pocock qualifies Fussner's thesis.

27. Sidney, *Defence*, 83, 84, 90, 85. Compare Wyman H. Herendeen, "Wanton Discourses and the Engines of Time: William Camden—Historian among Poets-Historical," in *Renaissance Rereadings: Intertext and Context*, ed. Maryanne Cline Horowitz, Anne J. Cruz, and Wendy A. Furman (Urbana, IL:

Univ. of Illinois Press, 1988), 147–8. Herendeen points to Sidney's historians to elucidate Camden's historiography in much the same way that I do to elucidate Spenser's.

28. Ferguson, *Clio*, 351. Ferguson's remarks on Spenser's historical method in *A View* throw light on Spenser's treatment of Arthurian myth and on his general historiographical perspective in *The Faerie Queene*:

> In his penetrating analysis of the situation in Ireland, . . . Edmund Spenser took time to explain the principles he used in his attempt to understand Irish culture. Recognizing the danger of relying on the Irish chronicles and the oral tradition on which they are based—'remembrance of bards, which use to forge and falsify every thing as they list'—he pointed out the need for supplementing such sources . . . by general reading among authors, ancient and modern. Out of these, together with 'comparison of times, likenesses of manners and customs, affinity of words and names, properties of natures and uses, resemblances of rites and ceremonies, monuments of churches and tombs, and many like circumstances, I do gather a likelihood of truth; not certainly affirming anything, but by conferring of times, languages, monuments and such like, I do hunt out a probability of things. . . .' No self-styled antiquary of that day ever put the methods of the new antiquarianism more succinctly than the author of the *Faerie Queene*. (83)

Ferguson quotes from *A View of the Present State of Ireland*, ed. W.L. Renwick (Oxford, 1970), 39.

29. Ferguson, *Clio*, 36.

30. Ferguson, *Clio*, 421. On Tudor antiquarianism, see T.D. Kendrick, *British Antiquity* (London: Methuen, 1950); May McKisack, *Medieval History in the Tudor Age* (Oxford: Clarendon Press, 1971). On the influence of antiquarianism on Tudor historiography, compare Joseph M. Levine, *Humanism and History: Origins of Modern English Historiography* (Ithaca, NY: Cornell Univ. Press, 1987), 73–106; D.R. Woolf, *Idea of History*, 3–44. Levine and Woolf see the influence of antiquarian study on the writing of history emerging later than Ferguson does; but, even if they are correct, an amateur antiquarian and myth-making poet like Spenser could have derived ideas about cultural myth and cultural change from various sources, including antiquarianism, before these sources began to influence mainstream historical writing.

31. Ferguson, *Clio*, 37–8. Ferguson notes, however, that most histories, even Bacon's and Camden's, remained true to the chroniclers' definition; in

his preface to his *History of Elizabeth* (1615), for instance, Camden apologizes "'for occasionally including matters not immediately related to policies of government'" (11). This statement is consistent with the views of Woolf and Levine (see n. 30, above). Compare Donald R. Kelley, "Elizabethan Political Thought," in *The Varieties of British Political Thought, 1500–1800*, ed. J.G.A. Pocock (Cambridge: Cambridge Univ. Press, 1993), 47–79.

32. See Michael O'Connell, *Mirror and Veil: The Historical Dimension of Spenser's* Faerie Queene (Chapel Hill: Univ. of North Carolina Press, 1977). To account for the importance of cultural myth in Spenser's allegorical treatment of history, O'Connell emphasizes "historical allusion," which allows multiple and mythic responses, instead of "historical allegory," which posits specific events and persons (11, cf. 87).

33. As implicit proof of Faeryland's relationship to Elizabethan England, Spenser tells several of those he addresses in the Dedicatory Sonnets—namely, Howard, Oxford, Hunsdon, Norris, and the Ladies of the Court—that they are "engrauen semblably" in the poem "Vnder a shady vele." Spenser's rhetorical strategy here includes an ironic dimension, for he argues that the "ydle rymes" of his "base Poeme," "the fruit of barren field," are nonetheless worthy to praise some of those whose favor the poet seeks; in other words, the poem builds an "euerlasting monument" to those whose censure it deserves (quotations from, respectively, sonnets to Howard, Oxenford, Hatton, Essex, Ormond, and Howard).

34. Nelson, *Fact and Fiction*, 1.

35. Nelson, *Fact and Fiction*, 81. Nelson (73, n. 1) cites studies of Spenser's humor; his chapter "Hobgoblin and Apollo's Garland" concerns Spenser's ironic play with distinctions between fact and fiction. See remarks on Renaissance pseudodocumentation in Nelson, 40, 80, and Robert Durling, *The Figure of the Poet in Renaissance Epic* (Cambridge: Harvard Univ. Press, 1965), 224. On the Proem to Book 2, compare A. Leigh Deneef, *Spenser and the Motives of Metaphor* (Durham, NC: Duke Univ. Press, 1982), 102–4. Murrin, *Allegorical Epic*, 137–9, takes Spenser seriously and, using "*Antiquitie* of *Faerie* lond" as proof, claims that Spenser "locates faery in India and finally in America" (see 2.9.60, 10.72).

Chapter II
Epic and Romance

Spenser creates three parallel nationalistic and exemplary quests representing three temporal perspectives on Tudor history; he constructs around Faeryland an innovative fictional world that enables the epic quests to commence and terminate in political history; and he invents a time-inclusive, allegorical world which, in coordination with the larger fictional world, allows the quests to evolve across time. He creates a subject matter, plot structure, and setting capable of accommodating the momentous heroic epic he never finished writing.

Upon the foundation of Virgilian epic, Spenser builds an expansive and many-storied temple to romance and allegory. He writes an allegorical romance epic, and he sets the main action of his poem in an imagined world that could serve as a glossary for the accumulated connotations of the word *romance* in Western literature. He presents an orderly, architectonic coordination of epic and romance that differs in form if not so much in matter from his major Italian models, Ariosto's *Orlando Furioso* and Tasso's *Gerusalemme Liberata*.[1] One of the formal distinctions between Spenser's poem and the Italians' concerns the structure of *The Faerie Queene*'s setting: Spenser creates spatial, temporal, ontological, and generic boundaries within his fictional world that have no counterparts in the Italian poems. These formal and relational boundaries derive in part from Spenser's medieval sources, from the ways he seeks to coordinate epic and romance, and from his decision to fashion a uniquely multiform representation of history.

Some remarks by C.S. Lewis in *The Allegory of Love* provide a useful perspective from which to view Spenser's structural innovation. After insisting on the intimate literary relationship between *The Faerie Queene* and Italian romance epic, Lewis turns to differences, claiming that "only the surfaces of the English and Italian poems are alike," only "what is first presented to our gaze—interlocked stories of chivalrous adventure in a world of marvels." He describes the fictional world of the *Orlando*, then summarizes before comparing that world to *The Faerie Queene*'s:

> Such is the Italian epic: in the foreground we have fantastic adventure, in the middle distance daily life, in the background a venerable legend with a core of momentous historical truth. There is no reason why the English poem should not have been much more like this than it actually is, if Spenser had chosen. Arthur's wars with the Saxons could have been worked up just as Boiardo and Ariosto worked up Charlemain's wars with the Saracens. The scene of the poem could have been laid in Britain and a real topography (as in the Italians) could have been used at every turn. . . . Ariosto begins with a situation—Roland's return from the East and Agramant's invasion of France. *The Faerie Queene* begins quite differently. A knight and a lady ride across our field of vision. We do not know where they are, nor in what period; the poet's whole energy is devoted to telling us what they look like. Ariosto begins like a man telling us, very well and clearly, a series of events which he has heard: Spenser begins like a man in a trance, or a man looking through a window, telling us what he sees. And however deep we dig in Spenser we shall never get to a situation, and never find a context in the objective world for the shapes he is going to show us.[2]

Lewis describes accurately not only relative differences in the subject matters but also differences in the quality of the experiences offered by the *Orlando* and *The Faerie Queene*. Lewis may even be right, in his way, about Faeryland's relationship to the "objective world." Yet it is precisely this "situation" and "context," the setting in history where Lewis says Spenser might have set his main action, that Lewis and other critics overlook or ignore in Spenser's poem. Spenser uses this situation for the same purpose as the Italians: to add to his poem the epic gravity of historical truth by founding his invention on a story from history and setting the story in a geographical context. Spenser differs from the Italians in the way he builds the world of political history into his poem. The center of Ariosto's fictional world is Paris under siege; the center of Tasso's, Jerusalem. It is to these places and these wars that the heroes return at intervals in the course of their fantastic adventures. Conversely, the center of Spenser's fictional world is Faeryland, around which various historical places and times form a frame. Like other heroic quests, Spenser's originate and were to have culminated in political history, but they develop within the boundaries of an imagined world. Spenser builds his poem upon historical situations in the political world; however, he creates geographical and generic boundaries between this world and Faeryland. He organizes his fictional world differently from the Italians and sets the main action in an invented allegorical world.

Even without the allegory, the sharp separation in *The Faerie Queene* between Faeryland and the places outside its borders has no counterpart in the Italian poems. Most of the action of the *Orlando* takes place in an undifferentiated chivalric forest not substantially unlike the Arthurian Broceliande or Spenser's Faeryland without the allegory. But Ariosto creates no boundaries between this forest and actual geography, between events there and events in the political world. Paris is a city within this forest, and even the most remarkable adventures take place within a recognizable geography. For example, Bradamante rescues Ruggiero from the enchanted castle of Atlante in the Pyrenees;[3] a moment after his rescue, Ruggiero sets off against his will on Atlante's flying horse. The griffin-horse takes him far to the west to Alcina's island in India (America) (6.10); after his adventures there, he rides the now tame horse the rest of the way around the world, and Ariosto provides a detailed record of his flight over Asia and Europe (10.58–60). Back in western Europe, Ruggiero spends some time in London (10.61–76), frees Angelica from chains on an island in the Irish Sea, and flies with her on the griffin-horse back to "little Britain" (10.94–5).[4] Spenser is also specific concerning the geographical places that compose his fictional world, but unlike Ariosto and Tasso he creates boundaries that are more than geographical between his imagined world of Faeryland and the fictionalized places outside it.

Spenser bases the distinction between Faeryland and the places representing political and religious history—Eden lands, Britain, Ireland, Cleopolis—on a distinction between romance and epic that he derives from classical and medieval literature. Outside Faeryland is the world of political conflict (war), ruled by the authority of a king or lord; in this world, a hero's earthly duty is directed exclusively toward historical destiny or a political leader. Faeryland is a world of individual conflict (erotic and ethical), limited only by the boundaries of imagination; here a hero's duty can afford, for a time, to be divided. Spenser's heroes feel the pressure of their quests, but their adventures in Faeryland evolve at a distance from external political control.[5] The characteristic activity in the world outside Faeryland represents the heroic subject matter, which imitates the most intense political experience—war; the characteristic activities within Faeryland represent the romance subject matters, which imitate the most intense personal experiences—conflicts in love and ethical conduct. Spenser's epic heroes, after confrontations with self in Faeryland, must serve political authority and historical destiny by fighting wars outside Faeryland.[6]

Italian Renaissance critics imply Spenser's distinction whenever they demand that epic narrative depict political history; however, because they base their distinctions between epic and romance primarily upon reactions to the *Orlando* or contrasts between the *Orlando* and the *Liberata*, they tend to emphasize differences between single and multiple plots, more or less probable actions, and lesser or greater degrees of fantastic imitation. Since both Ariosto and Tasso supply a core of political action and mingle heroic and romance adventures within their fictional worlds, their poems do not demand the same kind of formal distinction Spenser builds into his setting.[7] In *The Faerie Queene*, Britain and other places outside Spenser's imagined world stand in a relationship to classical and medieval heroic narrative as Faeryland does to the multifarious manifestations of romance.

The distinctions drawn in the previous paragraphs between romance and heroic narrative, between the subject matters of romance and epic, and between Faeryland and places outside of it must be understood as, at best, rough approximations that demand constant qualification and adjustment in response to the complexities of *The Faerie Queene* and other texts. Part of the problem is terminological,[8] but the larger issue concerns the relative incapacity of any critical terms to describe adequately the fathomless complexity of major literary texts. The most potent Western narratives, including, preeminently, the *Aeneid*, invite categorization, actively resist it, and, finally, assimilate all of it. These stories merge apparently incompatible materials and exploit the clashes and dialectical encounters between the interpretive strategies that seek to contain them. Anyone who employs a comprehensive term such as *epic* or, in the context of that term, attempts to interpret an enigmatic and magisterial text such as the *Aeneid* must be willing to qualify every assertion.

According to the generic terminology outlined above, Aeneas embraces epic heroism when he chooses to leave Dido and initiate imperial Roman history. Barbara Bono offers one kind of qualification to this assertion. She argues that the *Aeneid*'s epic scope and Aeneas's epic heroism depend not so much on the fact that Aeneas leaves Dido as on his acknowledgement of historical change and his awareness of the tragic, though ultimately triumphant, consequences of his actions. She sees in the *Aeneid* a thoroughgoing critique of Homeric heroism that focuses not on clear-cut distinctions but on dialectical tensions between versions of the heroic.[9] Nonetheless, while she analyzes various Renaissance responses to the problem of heroism in the *Aeneid*, most of which she sees as achieving some resolution of the tension that characterizes Virgil's poem, the perennial terms of the debate over epic heroism remain to trouble that resolution. In the figure of Britomart, Bono claims, Spenser can be seen "triumphantly assimilating classical epic in romance." Yet Britomart's eventual return to Britain represents a choice analogous to Aeneas's; she must finally choose between the alternatives in the list Bono attributes to the Renaissance debate over the *Aeneid*: "individual versus community, love versus duty, will versus reason, eros versus civilization, nature versus power."[10] Britomart, like Aeneas, must make the epic choice by participating in her historical destiny and espousing the second members of the list.

While admitting the limitations of the distinctions drawn in this book between epic and romance, I would also defend their relative usefulness and accuracy. To test this assertion with a radical example: if Aeneas had chosen (or had had the option of choosing) Dido instead of political conflict and passive Lavinia, the *Aeneid* could not have become the same kind of watershed of Western epic narrative that it did, for it would have ceased to be proto-imperial history and ceased to embody heroic and proto-Christian sacrifice, as it does. To take a more conventional example: those who defended the *Orlando* as romance were probably responding to the same aspects of the poem—including but not limited to its erotic preoccupations—as those who censured it as romance; and those who defended it as epic were probably responding to different aspects of it—particularly its political and dynastic concerns but also its moral didacticism. To take a final example: Western narrative fiction, particularly through the Renaissance, typically concerns love and war, desire and duty, erotic and heroic activities in which, in Christian narratives, God sometimes exerts an influence. Insofar as divine providence reflects imperial or dynastic claims, God takes part in epic; insofar as divine providence leads the individual on an internal pilgrimage toward spiritual fulfillment, God takes part in a religious embodiment of romance. Admittedly, generic classifications betray their own restricted efficacy, and terminological ambiguities persist, but such is the literary critical predicament.

Epic and romance may be distinguished by reference to cultural, religious, or literary history, by formal and stylistic analysis, or by their respective subject matters and settings. But the epic and romance impulses are constant in Western literature, and they find expression in two different kinds of narrative emphasis: a focus on war and national destiny and a focus on love and psycho-social awareness. The literary roots of the distinction lie, in part, in the Homeric subject matters: the tragic *Iliad* may be associated with epic and the comic *Odyssey* with romance.[11] The *Odyssey* is of course epic in scope, and it observes most of the conventions that have come to be associated with epic, but its subject matter—journeying, individual adventure in strange lands, final domestic reconciliation—makes it the literary foundation of the romance impulse in Western narrative fiction. Odysseus leaves the tragic wars in Troy and journeys in a setting immune to external political control; he is driven to endure not by the heroic code but by a desire to return to his wife and homeland, sustained not by rage and vengeance but by learning restraint and by the desire for order and domestic peace.

Virgil combines the Homeric subject matters and in doing so draws upon the norms of epic while introducing romance elements, such as Aeneas's Odyssean journeying, his passionate love for Dido, and his predisposition toward compassion. The *Aeneid* is not a romance; it is, indeed, the archetype of Western epic. Aware of the tragic consequences, Aeneas accepts his duty to historical destiny and the hard trials of nation-building, including the accompanying war. When he must, he fights with the rage of Achilles, and the final stroke that takes the life of Turnus expresses the heroic energy necessary to Aeneas's task. But the hesitation before the stroke, laden with tragic pathos, emphasizes the struggle within Aeneas between duty and desire that in part defines the difference between epic and romance. Again, Aeneas is not a romance hero, for he neither remains with Dido nor shirks his final duty; but he does hesitate before striking Turnus his death blow, and it is only his sudden awareness of the belt of Pallas on his enemy's shoulder that stirs his rage enough to move him to heroic action in the cause of defending his friend's honor.[12] Spenser uses the *Aeneid* to assert the epic foundations of his poem, but he also, implicitly, defends his unabashed embrace of romance by recognizing those aspects of Virgil's poem that came to be associated with romance.

Christian allegorical interpretations of the *Aeneid* revaluated the heroic poem as a spiritual manifestation of romance. Allegorical readings of the *Aeneid* exerted a strong influence on medieval narrative and on Spenser by stressing Christian themes that the commentators found implicit in Virgil's pagan and heroic narrative.[13] Aeneas became the fallen Everyman, who matures through wisdom after being purged of sin; his story could represent the successive ages of man or the individual soul's journey toward God. Interpreted in such a way, the *Aeneid* looks forward to the concerns of a new world—"to introspection, heart-searching, pity for one's enemy, doubt of the value of worldly success."[14] These themes exemplify some of the ideals of early Christianity, but they especially anticipate the revolutionary theology of Peter Abelard, St.

Bernard, and, later, St. Francis, theological perspectives that emphasize individual spiritual fulfillment, direct access to God's grace, and freedom from worldly authority in the name of the highest authority—the self in communion with God.[15]

Religious and partially secularized versions of the spiritual quest became the primary subject matter for medieval narrative. In its secular manifestations, the spiritual quest provided the occasion for the heroes of romance to seek individual fulfillment through love and adventure apart from the demands of any authority outside the self. The romance hero, like the epic hero, tests his courage and strength against any obstacle he confronts, but his tests are governed by chance, by providence, or by his own will, not by earthly authority or political events. The hero of romance avoids, either by choice or by chance, the final test of his mortality; he may be protected from death, like Gawain in *Gawain and the Green Knight*, or he may exist in a world in which death is not a real possibility. He chooses individual desire—for self-preservation, erotic love, or moral perfection—over any duty that might infringe upon it. Of course, the most sophisticated medieval romances often center on the conflicting loyalties inherent in the chivalric code, and most heroes owe allegiance not only to themselves but also to kings, lords, hosts, God, and the precepts of love and courtesy. Nonetheless, the heroes of romance are seldom required to sacrifice their lives in the name of external authority; they move in a world distanced from absolute political control.

Some of the major literary sources for the constitution of *The Faerie Queene*'s setting and for Spenser's manipulation of his quests include the texts that compose the Elizabethan medieval inheritance, the various streams of narrative literature that flow north out of an intellectually vital and innovative twelfth-century France.[16] To switch metaphors, the streams might be thought of as species of narrative; each species had been evolving long before the middle of the eleventh century, but all were recombined, supplemented, redirected, and quickened into new life during the years 1050–1200. A brief survey of these species as they evolve toward Spenser's immediate medieval sources is in order.

Three species evolve in a relatively direct line from the chivalric romances of Chrétien de Troyes. First, Chrétien's mimetic and symbolic depiction of the psychology of love finds allegorical expression in the *Roman de la Rose*,[17] which participates in the dream-vision species. Second, the Arthurian material, drawn from Celtic sources and chronicles and amplified by Chrétien and others, is codified and expanded in the thirteenth-century Cyclic Arthuriad or Vulgate Cycle, Malory's direct source.[18] Third, the work of Chrétien, Marie de France, Benoît de Sainte-Maure, and other writers of tales provided the impetus for the proliferation and dissemination of the species called metrical romance.[19] Also of significance for the study of Spenser are the voluminous didactic and hagiographic literatures: the literature of exemplum and sermon; and the saints' legends, often including visions of spiritual journeys, codified by Jacobus de Voragine during the mid-thirteenth century in the *Legenda Sanctorum* and printed by Caxton as *The Golden Legend.* The extensive vision and dream-vision literature, both secular and religious and most often allegorical, influenced Spenser directly through Guillaume de Lorris, Langland, Chaucer, and Lydgate, and probably accounts for the quality of the setting in Faeryland better than any other literary source.[20] Finally, ostensibly historical narrative takes various forms: annals and chronicles, of which Geoffrey of Monmouth's *Historia Regum Britanniae* is especially important to Spenser, continue to be produced; heroic narrative in the form of *gestes* continues to flourish after the twelfth century, and a great deal of legendary heroic material is incorporated into the metrical romances as the matters of France, Rome, Britain, England, and antiquity.

Spenser found in the chivalric romances and in the allegorical dream-visions—religious and secular, homiletic and erotic—fictional worlds and narrative structures that he put to work in *The Faerie Queene*. In the chivalric romances he found individual knights setting out on solitary quests in which they confront, often in symbolic settings, tests designed for them alone. In the dream-visions he found a similar narrative pattern and an extension of the same setting, individuals falling asleep and narratives that develop, by means of allegory, in the world of the individual mind. In *The Faerie Queene*, the setting of the chivalric quest in combination with that of the dream-vision became the model for the place Spenser calls Faeryland; similarly, the locale from which the knights in chivalric romance move out upon their quests (often Arthur's court) in combination with the setting of heroic narrative and the waking state in dream-vision became the model for the fictional world outside Faeryland.

Spenser probably knew neither *La Chanson de Roland* nor the romances of Chrétien de Troyes, but the distinctions he conceived between the fictional world outside Faeryland and Faeryland itself are analogous to the distinctions modern critics draw between the *Roland* and Chrétien's chivalric romances, and by extension between the heroic *chansons de geste* and the medieval romances generally. In *Mimesis*, Erich Auerbach provides a distinction that has become standard. He calls the *Roland* a heroic epic and argues that it, like other epics, "*is* history, at least insofar as it recalls actual historical conditions—however much it may distort and simplify them—and insofar as its characters always perform a historico-political function. This historico-political element is abandoned by the courtly novel, which consequently has a completely new relationship to the objective world of reality."[21] The courtly romances of the twelfth century "are entirely without any basis in political reality. The geographical, economic, and social conditions on which they depend are never explained." In the *chansons de geste* "a knight who sets off has an office and place in a politico-historical context"; the knight of Chrétien's romances serves no purpose "but that of self-realization."[22] Unlike the heroes of the *gestes*, who fight in wars, the heroes of romance seek feats of arms, single and isolated martial encounters that "do not fit into any politically purposive pattern." Love, rather than duty to a leader, motivates the romance knight's deeds of valor.[23] The experiences of Spenser's heroes in Faeryland do, ultimately, "fit into a politically purposive pattern," but the primary motivating force in Faeryland is love; and love, in combination with moral action, leads Spenser's heroes and readers toward self-awareness and the potential for self-fulfillment.

The knights of Arthurian chivalric romance set out on their adventures from a court that represents a world of social and political reality in which the heroes' lives are controlled by familial, tribal, political, and religious figures of earthly authority. The heroes' adventures lead them into a world in which the burden of authority falls upon them alone; they are guided by the power of their own intellects or by divine providence and preserved by the strength of their own wills or by the grace of God. In this world their beings are tested, defined, and transformed; they return changed to the world from which they had set forth. The basic plot structure of chivalric romance represents one formulation of the archetypal pattern of human myth, and it did not take modern psychologists and anthropologists to recognize the pattern. The components of the tripartite structure have many names: memory, understanding, will; wit, understanding, memory; action, contemplation, action; descent, illumination, ascent; corporeal substance, intellectual substance, judgment; emanation, conversion, return; idea, mind, soul; separation, initiation, return; crisis, confession and comprehension, transformation.[24]

Employing the basic plot structure of chivalric romance in combination with philosophical, theological, mythical, and psychological formulations of the archetypal pattern, Spenser fashions his quests in response to the archetype. The heroes of *The Faerie Queene* set forth from either Britain or Cleopolis, the former a representational depiction of sixth-century historical actuality, the latter an allegorical depiction of sixteenth-century and prophetic historical actuality; these are Spenser's equivalents to the Arthurian court of chivalric romance in combination with the traditional epic setting. Here the heroes receive their calls to adventure and are armed and instructed before proceeding on their quests.[25] Arthur experiences a dream-vision of the Faery Queen in sixth-century Britain (1.9.13–5); although the Faery Queen is gone when Arthur awakens, the vision remains alive in his mind; insofar as the setting in Faeryland represents the setting of dream-vision allegory, Faeryland is an extension of Arthur's visionary experience in Britain. Arthur dreams his desire and enters his dream to search for its source in Faeryland. Similarly, when Britomart gazes into Merlin's magic glass in Britain, she views her imagination in Faeryland (3.2.17–26); insofar as Faeryland mirrors imagination, it extends and redefines the image Britomart perceives in the "glassie globe" in her native land. Britomart imagines her desire in Britain and enters her imagination to seek the source of her desire in Faeryland. When Redcrosse, Guyon, Artegall, and Calidore move into Faeryland from Cleopolis, they enact analogous though—given the allegorical relationship between Cleopolis and Faeryland— less radical versions of Arthur's and Britomart's transformative experiences. In all, when Spenser's heroes enter Faeryland, they emerge out of versions of political reality into a composite allegorical romance realm, simultaneously a time-inclusive world of universal history, a mirror of Elizabethan England, an undifferentiated chivalric forest, a Celtic otherworld, a dream state, and an image of inner reality.

Once in Faeryland, each hero moves through a series of minor adventures toward major experiences of self-definition and ethical analysis—for readers as much as for characters—in places of heightened allegorical intensity. Although Redcrosse and Artegall exit Faeryland to accomplish the tasks assigned by Gloriana, none of the heroes truly completes the three-part mythic structure, for none reaches any definitive goal. Redcrosse never returns to marry Una in Eden lands, Britomart never returns to Britain with Artegall, and Arthur never reaches Cleopolis; rather, all Spenser's heroes end up stranded in Faeryland. As such, they may inhabit a poem whose stories never end, whose genres deny closure: allegory that produces apparently endless interpretation as readers and characters reach toward constantly deferred unity; romance that produces apparently endless dilation of being and narrative as readers and characters reach toward conclusive self-awareness, which continues to turn more and more deeply in upon itself;[26] and heroic epic narrative, most obviously end-dominated, that necessarily participates in the endless acquisitive desire of imperialism. So Spenser's heroes never finish with Faeryland, never make their way back to their final political confrontations; however, Spenser constructs a narrative that anticipates epic closure and creates a fictional world that could have accommodated those passages back, had they ever occurred. It is to a description of this fictional world that I now turn.

Notes
Chapter II

1. Spenser's debt to Tasso may not be as profound as his debt to Ariosto, but the orderly epic plan that Spenser outlines in the Letter to Ralegh participates in the neoclassical reaction to the *Orlando* that swept through Europe during the last half of the sixteenth century. Compare Fichter, *Poets Historical*, 205–6: "Perhaps more than anything else, the nature of Spenser's attitude toward wandering finally sets him apart from his Italian forerunners. He is neither so ready as Ariosto to make of vicissitude a matter of delight, to exploit it with whimsical perversity, nor so insistent as Tasso on censuring it. Spenser contemplates mutability with humility and patience." On Spenser's debt to Italian romance epic generally, see John Arthos, *On the Poetry of Spenser and the Form of Romances* (London: George Allen and Unwin, 1956), 92–183; and *Variorum*, 3: 367–76.

2. Lewis, *Allegory of Love*, 308–10.

3. Lodovico Ariosto, *Orlando Furioso*, trans. Sir John Harington (1591), ed. Graham Hough (Carbondale, IL: Southern Illinois Univ. Press, 1962), Book 4, stanza 8. All references to the *Orlando* are to this edition; they are cited in the text by book and stanza.

4. Ariosto's "Little Britain" is of course Brittany, as Spenser's "greater Britain" is Wales. One can hardly imagine a griffin-horse in Spenser's British setting, but it would not be out of place in Faeryland.

5. Gloriana is the nominal political ruler of Faeryland, but her direct control over events in Faeryland seems limited to being the catalyst for the services of a few often wayward knights. There is no law *per se* in Faeryland, no organized social structure, and no political conflict.

6. Insofar as dualistic models serve useful interpretive purposes, and with the provision that the binary concepts overlap, interpenetrate, and occupy the ends of spectrums, the following list offers some ideas associated with the terms *epic* and *romance*.

epic	*romance*
heroic	erotic
history	fiction
localized in time and space	unlocalized in time and space
autocratic	communal
public/political	private/personal
imperial/dynastic/martial	psycho-sexual/social

loyalty (service) to political group or leader	loyalty (service) to self and/or beloved
duty to external political authority	duty to self apart from external political control
most intense and conflict-ridden political experience	most intense and conflict-ridden interpersonal experience
war	love
duty	desire
hunt/conquest	search/compromise
male/phallic	female/yonic
extension/linear	dilation/cyclical
aggression as death instinct	aggression as sex instinct
intrusion/rape	immersion/emasculation
release in death	release in orgasm
climax—destruction and death (annihilation)	climax—sexual union and life (generation, reconciliation)
tragic	comic
end-dominated/closure	process-dominated/openness

7. On thematic aspects in Ariosto and Tasso analogous to Spenser's formal distinction between epic and romance, see Fichter, *Poets Historical*, 70–90; Margaret W. Ferguson, *Trials of Desire: Renaissance Defenses of Poetry* (New Haven: Yale Univ. Press, 1983), 69; David Quint, *Origin and Originality in Renaissance Literature: Versions of the Source* (New Haven: Yale Univ.Press, 1983), 92; Helgerson, *Forms*, 44–52; Javitch, *Proclaiming*, *passim*.

8. The terms *epic* and *romance* are conflict-ridden and ambiguous to begin with, so any use of them must begin with that fact. *Epic* is especially a problem, partly because it remains, in some quarters, as it has since the Renaissance, a term of value to name those long, ambitious poems the critic most admires. It also names those poems that self-consciously employ the traditional epic conventions: structural unity, "realistic" imitation, formal invocations, narrative flashbacks, divine interventions, grand themes involving dominant cultural norms, epic catalogues and similes, etc. According to a long tradition, *epic*, like *romance*, also refers to distinct subject matters (see n. 6, above), which is the way I often choose to use the term as a modifier, although perhaps *heroic*, which I also use, better serves to describe subject matter. But that creates its own problems. I use *romance* rather than *romantic* except when referring to erotic desire.

9. Barbara J. Bono, *Literary Transvaluation: From Vergilian Epic to Shakespearian Tragicomedy* (Berkeley: Univ. of California Press, 1984), 7–40. John M. Steadman, *Milton and the Renaissance Hero* (Oxford: Clarendon

Press, 1967), 1–22, offers a comprehensive overview of the various manifestations of epic heroism descending from Homer and Virgil to Milton, focusing on the debate between "poetic and philosophical patterns of heroic virtue" (9). Although Renaissance commentators accepted various kinds of heroic virtue as legitimate, including "love as a heroic formula" (12), most demanded martial competence (6–9), and Milton objects mightily. But everything changes with Milton, for once Satan becomes the embodiment of traditional epic heroism, all the old bets are off, although I can imagine Adam the romance hero perfectly at home in Faeryland. Concerning qualifications of traditional views of epic, see Mihoko Suzuki, *Metamorphoses of Helen: Authority, Difference, and the Epic* (Ithaca: Cornell Univ. Press, 1989), who takes issue with the usual assumption that men's heroic quarrels motivate epic action. She notes, accurately, that quarrels over women motivate epic; but, I would argue, the natures and outcomes of those arguments, as well as which women the men end up embracing, propel the poems toward epic or romance (on Aeneas and Dido, see 92–149; on Britomart and Artegall, see 150–209).

10. Bono, *Transvaluation*, 3,4; for more on Britomart, see 61–82.

11. The distinction is widespread in the Renaissance and is implicit in Spenser's distinction in the Letter to Ralegh between political and private virtues in reference to Homer's poems: "first Homere, who in the Persons of Agamemnon and Vlysses hath ensampled a good gouernour and a vertuous man, the one in his Ilias, the other in his Odysseis."

12. Virgil, *Aeneid*, trans. Frank O. Copley, 2nd ed. (Indianapolis: Bobbs-Merrill, 1975), 12.935–52:

> 'Return me—or if you will, my lifeless corpse—
> to my home. You've won; all Italy saw me beaten
> and on my knees; Lavinia is your wife.
> Press your ill will no further.' Aeneas checked
> a savage blow; his eye wavered, he halted;
> his hesitation had grown with every word.
> Just then at shoulder-peak he saw the baldric,
> proclaimed by clasp and shining studs the belt
> of Pallas, the lad whom Turnus fought and killed:
> he wore it—spoils of the fallen, an ill-starred prize.
> Aeneas, seeing the trophy, felt fierce pangs
> revive; a flame of fury and dreadful rage
> flared up; 'Shall you escape, dressed in the spoils
> of those I loved? No! Pallas wounds you here;
> he spills your blood as price and expiation!'

So saying, with savage thrust he sank the blade
in Turnus' heart: his limbs fell cold in death;
his life, with a curse and a moan, fled down to hell.

13. On Spenser's debt to the allegorical commentaries on the *Aeneid*, see Don Cameron Allen, *Mysteriously Meant: The Rediscovery of Pagan Symbolism and Allegorical Interpretation in the Renaissance* (Baltimore: Johns Hopkins Univ. Press, 1970), 103–54; Thomas E. Maresca, *Three English Epics: Studies of* Troilus and Criseyde, The Faerie Queene, *and* Paradise Lost (Lincoln: Univ. of Nebraska Press, 1979), 1–73; Murrin, *Allegorical Epic*, 3–50.

14. Tillyard, *English Epic*, 87.

15. On the relationship between twelfth-century theology and romance, see R.W. Southern, *The Making of the Middle Ages* (New Haven: Yale Univ. Press, 1953), 219–57.

16. The idea of a twelfth-century renaissance was first proposed by W.P. Ker in his pioneering and influential study, *Epic and Romance* (1896). Ker defends a thesis that links differences between epic and romance to political, religious, and literary changes during the eleventh and twelfth centuries, marking the end of the heroic age and the beginning of the chivalric. He compares the events of twelfth-century France to those of fourteenth-century Italy some thirty years before the classic account of this thesis by Charles Homer Haskins in *The Renaissance of the Twelfth Century* (Cambridge: Harvard Univ. Press, 1927). What Ker does for secular, non-allegorical narrative, Haskins does for Latin writings and the culture they mirrored and produced. The theses of Ker and Haskins have been debated and modified, but the basic changes described by these authors—in politics, economics, literature, the plastic arts, religion, and philosophy—form the foundation for much modern study in English of medieval art and culture.

Ker mentions most of the elements of medieval romance contained in modern definitions. He finds its literary roots in classical and Celtic sources and in Provençal lyric; he emphasizes the themes of love and chivalric adventure as they come to dominate narrative, to the exclusion of the heroic themes of the *chansons de geste*; he notes the innovative use of psychological description as a narrative tool; and he points to variety of incident, remoteness of scene, and marvelous occurrences as characteristic aspects of medieval romance (323–39).

17. See Lewis, *Allegory of Love*, 112–56. The *Roman de la Rose*, either in the original French or in Chaucer's translation, was one of the germinal books for Spenser's allegorical treatment of love.

18. See Eugene Vinaver, *The Rise of Romance* (Oxford: Clarendon Press, 1971), for a fascinating account of the evolution of the Arthurian matter through Malory.

Spenser may in fact have been influenced by *Le Morte Darthur* more than his few direct borrowings suggest. Malory sets out to tell one story, the story of Arthur; but between Arthur's birth, kingship, vast and successful conquests, and marriage (Books 1–5) and the story of the final conflicts leading to his downfall (Books 20–21), Malory tells five separate but related stories of chivalric adventure. Each of the five secondary stories—of Launcelot, Gareth, Tristram, the Grail, and Launcelot and Guinevere—includes one or more themes and incidents that become implicated in Arthur's downfall. In addition, the fifteen books that compose the five stories tell separate tales of chivalric adventure related both to the secondary stories of which they are parts and to the primary story of Arthur. This is the structure of Spenser's narrative as he outlines it in the Letter to Ralegh, and I can think of no other possible source than Malory. Arthur's is Spenser's controlling story, but each of the six books has its own story to tell, and each book contains other tales or, as Spenser says in the Letter, "particular purposes or by-accidents therein occasioned." These tales are "occasioned" because they are allegorically related to the stories of the books in which they appear, which are in turn related to the story of Arthur since the virtues associated with the five major heroes (Book 4 lacks a central hero) represent aspects of Arthur's magnificence.

Spenser writes an allegory in verse, Malory a representational and symbolic prose narrative; and Spenser reverses Malory's story by causing each successive book to glorify Arthur rather than lead to his downfall (though he adds a tragic Arthur in Artegall). However, the narrative and thematic structures of the two works are strikingly similar.

19. There are approximately sixty extant English metrical romances, many of them expanded or reduced translations from French originals. They are the most varied collection of tales imaginable. Some are chivalric, some truly heroic, some based on legendary history, some purely fantastic; there are homilies, saints legends, myths, and fairy tales among them. They include wars, visions, monsters, demons, divine intervention, allegory, and homely realism. Dieter Mehl, *The Middle English Romances of the Thirteenth and Fourteenth Centuries* (New York: Barnes and Noble, 1969), 252, provides as close an approximation to a definition as possible: "In Middle English, 'romance' in its widest sense includes everything that calls itself a tale and cannot strictly be classed as a historical chronicle or a saint's legend." These tales continued to be produced through the sixteenth century, and Spenser probably knew more of them than is usually assumed.

20. On Spenser's debt to Langland, see Judith H. Anderson, *The Growth of a Personal Voice*: Piers Plowman *and* The Faerie Queene (New Haven: Yale Univ. Press, 1976). She notes that at climactic moments in both poems "personality achieved becomes reality possessed" (127).

Lewis, *Allegory of Love*, 275–92, sees in the work of John Lydgate, Stephen Hawes, and Gavin Douglas a "fusion of erotic and homiletic allegory" with chivalric romance (287). The picture conjured up by this merging, of a morally exemplary knight and lover seeking adventures in an allegorical setting, depicts the life of Faeryland more completely than any other literary analogue. See also Tillyard, *English Epic*, 175, who compares Lydgate's chivalric and religious dream-allegory, the *Pilgrimage*, to *The Faerie Queene*. Merritt Y. Hughes, *Virgil and Spenser* (Berkeley: Univ. of California Press, 1929), 268, quotes Gabriel Harvey, who saw a direct line of descent from Chaucer, through Lydgate, to Spenser.

21. Erich Auerbach, *Mimesis: The Representation of Reality in Western Literature*, trans. Willard Trask (Princeton: Princeton Univ. Press, 1953), 122.

22. Auerbach, 133, 133, 134.

23. Auerbach, 140, 141. Most critics of medieval romance after Auerbach take his distinction for granted. Robert W. Hanning, *The Individual in Twelfth-Century Romance* (New Haven: Yale Univ. Press, 1977), 4–5, provides an expansion of Auerbach's thesis that seems particularly relevant to Spenser: "By investigating . . . the tensions between love and prowess . . . the chivalric romance makes of its adventure plot the story, nay the celebration, of the necessity of men (and women) to face the fact of their private destiny, and to attempt to attain that vision which . . . makes of life a process of dynamic self-realization. . . . Given this basic orientation, the chivalric poets felt free to treat the fact of individual destiny, and the necessity of seeking it by sacrificing the stability of an externally imposed order for the adventure of self-definition, from widely different points of view. Adapting and manipulating the conventions of chivalry, they placed their heroes in divergent, contradictory situations, not simply for the joy of showing mastery of a chosen form, but to explore and expose the *risks* of individuality."

24. Among the sources for the terms I supply, see Joseph Campbell, *The Hero with a Thousand Faces* (Cleveland: World Publishing, 1956), passim; Northrop Frye, *Anatomy of Criticism: Four Essays*, (Princeton: Princeton Univ. Press, 1957) 131–239; Maresca, *Three English Epics*, 13–4; Paul Piehler, *The Visionary Landscape: A Study in Medieval Allegory* (Montreal: McGill-Queen's Univ. Press, 1971), 19; John Stevens, *Medieval Romance: Themes and Approaches* (London: Hutchinson Univ. Press, 1976), 16–20.

25. Most critics do not notice Spenser's three-part quest patterns because they assume that all the action takes place in Faeryland. Tillyard,

English Epic, makes a telling statement in this regard. He argues that Spenser "does not altogether fulfill the choric function of true epic" (293) because "[o]rdinary people will put up with and admire large measures of the extraordinary if it is reached from an ordinary beginning. They want their heroes first to have their home among them and then to set out on their lonely expeditions and strange adventures" (292). This "ordinary beginning" is exactly what Spenser provides in Britain.

See Graham Hough, *A Preface to* The Faerie Queene (New York: W.W. Norton, 1962), 23; and John Erskine Hankins, *Source and Meaning in Spenser's Allegory: A Study of* The Faerie Queene (Oxford: Clarendon Press, 1971), 34; both point to Cleopolis as analogous to Arthur's court in Malory and chivalric romance.

26. See Teskey, "Allegory," 17; and Patricia Parker, *Inescapable*, 54–113, on, respectively, allegory and romance.

Chapter III
The Epic World of *The Faerie Queene*

Verisimilitude and poetic decorum demand that the setting of an epic poem be consistent in time and place with the historical subject matter. *The Faerie Queene* is especially susceptible to breaches of decorum in this area for two reasons: first, it is the only epic in the classic line whose dominant setting is an imaginary world; second, its composite historical narrative includes several temporal perspectives on Tudor history—a biblical, a sixth-century, a sixteenth-century, and a prophetic perspective, among others. Spenser achieves consistency between subject matter and setting by creating a multiform fictional world capable of accommodating a variety of spatial and temporal realms. Specific historical times and places outside Faeryland, in coordination with the time-inclusive medium of Faeryland, create a consistent anatomy of British history. The epic quests originate and were to have concluded outside Faeryland in the heroic epic world of political history; but the quests develop, and their heroes prepare for their historic roles, within the allegorical romance world of Faeryland. To understand the relation of history to *The Faerie Queene* and to appreciate Spenser's careful structuring of the epic quests, one must view the world of the poem from a perspective broader than Faeryland. Nonetheless, such understanding may best proceed from a recognition of Spenser's achievement in creating Faeryland, where most of the poem's action occurs.

1. Faeryland: The Verisimilar Fiction

When critics attempt to characterize the fictional world of *The Faerie Queene*, "the universe of discourse in which the poem unfolds,"[1] to borrow a phrase from Isabel MacCaffrey, most treat it as a single entity and interpret it according to the manner outlined by Robert Scholes and Robert Kellogg in their comprehensive and still useful book *The Nature of Narrative*: "Meaning, in a work of narrative art, is a function of the relationship between two worlds: the fictional world created by the author and the 'real' world, the apprehendable universe."[2] Since critics of *The Faerie Queene* almost invariably consider Faeryland coextensive with the world of the poem, they generally define the meaning of Spenser's fiction by delineating contrasts between Faeryland and quotidian reality. Recent historicist critics, who view "reality," including the poet's reality and even the language he employs, as an ideological construct, tend to collapse the distinction between fiction and actuality; in doing so, they presume to provide a more politically aware reading than those critics who see an idealized Faeryland as Spenser's representation of a stable, unified, and hierarchical providential design. John Bender might have been either old-fashioned or proto-historicist when, in 1972, he wrote that "ceremonial life at Elizabeth's court" would have "narrowed the gulf between ordinary experience and Spenser's fiction for many of his first readers."[3] For most critics, who associate Faeryland with some sort of ideal realm and emphasize its distance from the real world, reality comprises instability, uncertainty, and constant human error in a fallen world governed by the fickle hand of fortune.[4] While recent criticism—and in this revisions of revisionist historicism, including materialist feminism, stake their worthy claim—has sought to remedy the traditional propensity toward over-idealization of Spenser's invented world, the tendency persists, and it distorts the nature of Spenser's fiction. Faeryland is neither an idealized portrait of ideologically-sanctioned ethical conduct nor, worse, a prelapsarian (or not) golden world, though it is some of each of these; rather, it is an allegorical image of mortal existence that stresses the limitations, paradoxes, and uncertainties of human life while nevertheless offering irony and joy. Spenser creates in Faeryland a verisimilar complement to the historical fiction of his epic. As an entrance into this view of Faeryland, I revive some critical voices that have been all but drowned out by the current din of theory.

In her 1937 book *The Meaning of Spenser's Fairyland*, Isabel Rathborne offers what remains one of the most comprehensive and consistent explorations by analogy of *The Faerie Queene*'s fictional world. She identifies

Faeryland with a "heroes' paradise" or "land of fame, resembling the classical Elysium."[5] Rathborne's conception can account not only for *The Faerie Queene*'s multiple relation to history—the Britons are visitors to the land of the dead—but also for the apparently mortal forces of evil that inhabit, and all but dominate, Faeryland, for "there is good fame and ill fame," and "the types of evil which history preserves as warnings generally appear in classical pictures of the otherworld . . . as inhabiting a country near the abode of the blessed." Spenser simply merges the two places in order to allow Faeryland "to exhibit virtue in action."[6]

Rathborne shows how the traditional conception of Elysium can explain the presence of evil in Faeryland, but she admits the limitations of the classical analogue. Unlike the inhabitants of Elysium, Spenser's heroes display human strengths and weaknesses, and Faeryland is a "theater of heroic action," not a "static place of rewards and punishments."[7] Consequently, Rathborne widens the scope of her conception by introducing fairy mythology from folklore and romance, which provides a basis for a land of the dead or otherworld in which "heroes live lives closely resembling their heroic lives on earth." An inconsistency persists, however, for when Rathborne outlines life in Faeryland, she describes an existence quite different from that which confronts Spenser's heroes: it is, she says, "still the life of that heroic age which succeeded the age of gold and still partook of its splendors. [Faeryland] is not a peaceful world, nor a world without evil, but it is a happy world, for in it virtue is always triumphant."[8]

A world in which virtue is always triumphant—not just finally as in the Christian dispensation, but immediately and on every occasion triumphant—is a different place from the "state of mortall men" where "blisse may not abide" (1.8.44) that Spenser depicts in Faeryland. Unlike the heroes Rathborne describes, who inhabit a world of past and future, but not present, history, Spenser's heroes confront, at every turn in their ways through Faeryland, a problematical earthly existence:

> So tickle be the termes of mortall state
> And full of subtile sophismes, which do play
> With double senses, and with false debate,
> T'approue the vnknowen purpose of eternall fate.
>
> (3.4.28)

The perfectly ordered lives of the heroes Rathborne describes bear little resemblance to the error-ridden, confusing, and often painful lives of Spenser's heroes. Even Arthur, the exemplar of knighthood who suffers but seldom errs, laments the mutable and mortal nature of his life in Faeryland:

"So feeble is mans state, and life vnsound, / That in assurance it may neuer stand, / Till it dissouled be from earthly band" (2.11.30). Spenser's heroes, Briton and Faery alike, often make mistakes, even when reason seems to be guiding them; sometimes, when they are well aware, they approach experience cautiously, conscious of its often deceptive nature; in any case, they undergo trials designed to test the validity and efficacy of an ethical ideal when it confronts the dangerous and fickle "termes of mortall state." Faeryland is not a golden world of prelapsarian, ideal, or immortal existence; rather, it is a verisimilar imitation of mortal life, an allegorical medium that duplicates conscious and unconscious experience.[9]

Harry Berger, introducing an original and influential concept, compares Faeryland with other Renaissance "second world[s] . . . set over against the first world created by God," worlds that create in the careful reader "a dialectical awareness of the tensions and interrelationships between fiction and actuality."[10] Berger takes issue with Frye's too exclusive description of Faeryland as a "green world," pointing out that the second world or "heterocosm" is a dynamic creation more inclusive and complex than Frye's green world: "The particular virtue of the imaginary world lies in the fact that, since it is neither actual nor ideal, it is potentially an image of either or both."[11]

Spenser creates an internally consistent mirror of reality in Faeryland by supplementing references to history, physical nature, and social existence with verisimilar imitations of worlds within the mind. As a number of critics suggest, Faeryland reflects various aspects of the innerworld: dream, prophecy, vision, imagination, cultural myth, the state of the soul, psychological reality, and the world of poetry within the poet's mind.[12] As a mirror of waking existence, Faeryland depicts states of the mind or soul by recording cognitive and psychological processes: the thoughts and desires of the heroes are played out and revealed in the narrative. Settings, characters, beasts, and events representing various conditions of the psyche dramatize a psychomachia.[13] Working along similar lines, Isabel MacCaffrey constructs an analogue for Faeryland capable of truly representing the variety and inclusiveness of Spenser's imagined world: "Fairy Land 'is' the human imagination itself, hospitable to solicitations from the world without and the world within. . . . The reader who enters the world of *The Faerie Queene* assents to a journey within, which yet leaves nothing behind or 'outside' that he would wish to retain."[14] In Faeryland, as in the imagination, seeming inconsistencies of time and space are reconciled within a world that may include the whole of history, the total potential of mind and will, past mistakes, present desires, future glories.[15]

Spenser allows his fiction to reflect multiple images of reality in a variety of different ways by employing various degrees of allegory, which extend across a spectrum from representational to allegorical fictional modes. As Lewis points out, "not everything in the poem is equally allegorical, or even allegorical at all. We shall find that it is Spenser's method to have in each book an allegorical core, surrounded by a margin of what is called 'romance of types,' and relieved by episodes of pure fantasy."[16] Scholes and Kellogg note that "the characters range from generalized types of the actual to stipulated symbols illustrative of abstract ideas."[17] Rosemond Tuve is more radical in imposing limits on Spenser's allegory; she insists that Spenser explicitly "tells" us when he expects his narrative, iconography, or characters to be read allegorically; most of the time he is telling an unallegorical romance story. At the same time, Tuve admits that there are degrees of allegorical intent between the two poles.[18]

MacCaffrey examines two kinds of allegory in *The Faerie Queene*: "analytic allegory" concerns "'this temporal life'" and "the psychic processes of fallen man," while "synthetic allegory" concerns "'that eternal life'" and "the human soul's awareness of its permanent alternatives: Heaven and Hell, felicity and damnation." This distinction, MacCaffrey contends, is inherent in the language itself: the temporal and the eternal "exist in a counterpoint which Spenser's readers apprehend as an alteration between different fictional techniques, or different versions of metaphor." Analytic and synthetic allegory represent, for MacCaffrey, the poles of a spectrum whose references reach from the temporal to the eternal: the allegorical spectrum comprises "different versions of metaphor" whose places on the spectrum reflect the distance between the tenor and vehicle of the trope. The distance is least in the analytic and greatest in the synthetic, in which the tenor is most distinct from human experience. Analytic allegory depicts the earthly and horizontal dimension of existence by means of "'unfolded'" images; synthetic allegory depicts the "visionary or vertical dimension" by means of allegorically intense "'infolded'" images that "imitate a complex simultaneity of experience associated with mystical rapture and poetic inspiration."[19] As MacCaffrey knows, most of Spenser's allegory belongs in the area between the poles and points in both directions; thus, she finds herself speaking of degrees of "ontological energy"[20] in reference to particular episodes, characters, images, and settings.

The terminology MacCaffrey adopts in her analysis of Spenser's allegory provides one means of describing distinctions among settings in Faeryland. For example, she associates the "'infolded'" images of synthetic allegory with places such as the Mount of Contemplation, the Garden of Adonis, and the Temple of Isis, "where the poem's atmosphere thickens and illumination dims." These places are "anagogic, pointing to some version of conclusiveness"; they are what Spenser would probably have called his darkest conceits, "opaque complex images" which, paradoxically, give way to "unanalyzed transparency."[21] They are the same places that Lewis refers to as "allegorical core[s]," places of heightened allegorical intensity that define the upper ontological limits of Faeryland. These include, for Lewis, the House of Holiness, Alma's castle, the Garden of Adonis, the Temple of Venus, the Church of Isis, and Mount Acidale. At the opposite end of the ontological spectrum, Spenser furnishes demonic counterparts to the allegorical cores: the dungeon of Orgoglio; the caves of Error, Despair, Ate, and Malengin; and the houses of Mammon and Busirane. The narrative of Faeryland unfolds between these ontological poles, and each place in Faeryland occupies a location on a spectrum extending from divine to demonic states of being. Certain of the ontological poles represent as well cosmological poles that establish some of the spatial limits of Spenser's imagined world. Any place higher than the Mount of Contemplation or Mount Acidale or deeper than the lowest extent of the House of Mammon exists not in Faeryland but, respectively, in the heavens or in Hades.[22]

Incorporating MacCaffrey's terminology into a comprehensive map of *The Faerie Queene*'s setting, I would describe the universe of the poem as including a horizontal dimension of "analytic" allegory and a vertical dimension of "synthetic" allegory. The horizontal—the spatial and temporal terrestrial setting in the fallen world—intersects the vertical—the topographical and cosmological setting situated between heaven and hell—on the plain in Faeryland where much of the action occurs. Vertical shifts in the setting—up a mountain, down into a valley or cave, up or down into a building—reflect changes in the ontological status of the events portrayed, usually accompanied by an increase in allegorical intensity roughly proportional to the distance of a particular setting from the plain. Thus, MacCaffrey's single vertical allegorical and ontological axis—from divine to demonic—divides at the horizontal plane (plain) into two parts representing two spectrums of allegorical intensity and ontological being, two movements from analysis to synthesis: one extends upward from the "analytic" to the divine "synthetic," and one extends downward from the "analytic" to the demonic "synthetic." Places and events within Faeryland and outside Faeryland may be located, more or less roughly, at points representing intersections of the horizontal and vertical axes. In what follows, I focus on locations outside Faeryland.

2. The Larger World of the Poem

Most of the action of *The Faerie Queene* takes place in Faeryland, but some of it takes place outside Faeryland, in the larger cosmic and terrestrial universe that Spenser builds to house his epic. Spenser situates Faeryland in a syncretic yet traditional epic cosmos that reaches from heaven to hell, and he constructs a terrestrial geography around Faeryland that conforms to the traditional heroic setting. Every place outside Faeryland corresponds to a particular part of the Christian/pagan cosmology or to a particular place and time in political or religious history. Harry Berger notes that Faeryland "seems to have two references: to [Spenser's] own literary world of the imagination, the myths and fictions devised by the poet of *The Faerie Queene*; and to . . . the fictions, myths, and legends recorded throughout history."[23] Berger is right; Faeryland does have these two references. But within the larger fictional universe that includes Faeryland, imagined fictions and imitations of interior worlds exist in Faeryland, while imitations of the known cosmos and transparent representations of historical times and places exist outside Faeryland.

The Epic Cosmos

In conformity with epic tradition, Spenser sets his poem in a cosmos larger than earth. Frye provides one kind of cosmic diagram for *The Faerie Queene*: "there is a heaven above, referred to in a very few passages; . . . then a world of 'Faerie,' where the main action of the poem takes place; then the world of history and ordinary experience, described obliquely through allegory; and then a demonic world from which monsters and other sinister creatures emerge."[24] I would argue that the world of history exists both obliquely or darkly in Faeryland and explicitly or transparently in the larger fictional world outside Faeryland, but Frye's outline of the cosmic realms is accurate. MacCaffrey notes that "Spenser's road in *The Faerie Queene* winds not only 'through places of the soul,' but through fictive places that point toward or stand for actual locations in the macrocosm, to wit, Heaven, Hell, and the wilderness of this world."[25] Journeys to underworld realms outside Faeryland occur on several occasions. Archimago sends one of the infernal spirits he commands to Morpheus' house, "Amid the bowels of the earth" (1.1.39); Agape visits the Fates, "Downe in the bottome of the deepe *Abysse*" (4.2.47); and Duessa travels with Night through Hades itself to bring the wounded Sansjoy to Aesculapius (1.5.31-41). None of the action of *The Faerie Queene* takes place in the Christian heaven, but the divine world is invoked three times: in Redcrosse's vision from the Mount of Contemplation (1.10.55-6), in the angel's appearance as protector of Guyon after he faints (2.8.5-8), and in the final stanzas of the *Mutabilitie Cantos*, where Spenser prays to the supreme Being behind Nature herself (7.8.1-2).

Just below the Christian heaven in the world of *The Faerie Queene* is a place corresponding to the heavens of classical myth and epic—the native habitat of the gods or, as MacCaffrey says, "the home of Milton's Attendant Spirit."[26] The narrative includes several journeys to this realm. Disgusted with a sin-ridden world and "loathing lenger here to space / Mongst wicked men," Astraea "Return'd to heauen, whence she deriu'd her race"; she is "now," Spenser says, the constellation Virgo, whose power influences the whole created universe (5.1.11). Spenser is even more explicit about Mutabilitie's ascent from earth: she travels "past the region of ayre, / And of the fire" "to the Circle of the Moone," then up "through the purest sky / To Ioues high Palace" (7.6.7,8,23). Similarly, Cymoent leaves the "watry gods," ascends "Vnto the shinie heaven," and brings back Apollo to cure Marinell (4.12.25).

As might be expected, Venus also does some transcosmic traveling in *The Faerie Queene*. Having lost Cupid, she leaves "her heauenly hous / The house of goodly formes and faire aspects," to search the earth for him (3.6.12). She seeks him at court, in cities, in the country, and finally in "the saluage woods and forrests wyde," where she searches "the secret haunts of Dianes company" (3.6.13-6). She travels everywhere and exists everywhere, for such is the nature of her influence. She leaves a place that is ontologically and spatially distinct from Faeryland and searches for Cupid in the wider earth of the poem, the whole fallen world of which Faeryland is a part. She searches a court unlike the courts of Faeryland, whether Malecasta's, Alma's, or Gloriana's, primarily because it appears to be unallegorical (see 3.6.13). Venus next searches cities, which must include places outside Faeryland, for Faeryland has only one city, Cleopolis (see 3.6.14). She then goes to the country, and the pastoral setting suggests a closer approach to Faeryland. Finally, when Venus enters the "saluage woods," she seems to be moving into a typical Faeryland setting. But this is not explicitly Faeryland; rather, it is "the secret haunts of Dianes company" (3.6.16).

Spenser seems intentionally ambiguous concerning the relation of immortals generally and Venus in particular to his imagined world. In the present case, after Venus convinces Diana to assist in her search for Cupid, the two explore "the wilderness" (3.6.10), where they come upon Chrysogone giving birth to Amoret and Belphoebe. Venus and Diana kidnap the infants, and in the very next stanza Venus takes Amoret to one of the least localized settings in the poem—the Garden of Adonis—where, as MacCaffrey maintains, "microcosm and macrocosm are superimposed."[27] Berger contends that as we move toward the Garden, "we move from the temporal succession of the narrative to the lyric moment of the garden, a place in the imagination where the strands and fragments may be, as it were, organized into a simultaneous 'spatial' unity."[28] To approach this place Spenser guides his reader, in the space of a dozen or so stanzas, out of the heavens, through a fairly stark representation of the actual world, into a relatively idealized rural setting, on toward the unlocalized haunts of Diana, and finally to a mythic place where an immaculate conception and a painless delivery occur. From there it is a short step to the Garden of Adonis itself, wherever it may be: "Whether in *Paphos*, or *Cytheron* hill, / Or it in *Gnidus* be, I wote not well," Spenser admits (3.6.29). Venus may be the presiding pagan deity of *The Faerie Queene*, but Spenser seems to want to keep her and other immortals distanced from the mortal world of Faeryland. The other two places where Venus is specifically invoked are apposite. Significantly, both are allegorical cores: she appears at the Court of Venus in Book 4, where she is veiled (10.40-1), and she is implicitly invoked on Mt. Acidale in Book 6 (10.12), where Colin's "lasse" supplants both her and Elizabeth (10.16; see 10.25-8).

The ambiguous relation of the classical deities to Faeryland is an instance of the distinction Berger draws between the two references of Faeryland, the one to Spenser's "own literary world of the imagination" and the other to "the fictions, myths, and legends recorded throughout history."[29] If, as I believe, Spenser reserves Faeryland for his own myths and fictions, he would, logically, exclude the creations of classical myth from his invented world. Furthermore, as planetary and astrological forces, the gods influence all of created existence; therefore, Spenser emphasizes their relationships to a larger universe that includes Faeryland and the larger fictional earth of the poem as well as the actual cosmos. The goddess Mutabilitie is a case in point: "all the worlds fair frame . . . / She alter'd quite," perverting "all which Nature had establisht first / In good estate" and all which "God had blest" (7.6.5). Since, as Lewis states, she represents "the force behind the sin of Adam,"[30] the result of her influence is a Christian historical fact: hers is the "pittous worke . . . / By which, we all are subiect to that curse, / And death in stead of life haue sucked from our Nurse" (7.6.6). As a hard fact of mortal existence, Mutabilitie is at work in Faeryland and in the larger fictional world, but insofar as she influences the course of actual human history, Spenser distances her from Faeryland.

All the action of the *Mutabilitie Cantos* takes place outside Faeryland. Mutabilitie leaves the fallen earth and ascends to Jove's court. Later, when the gods return to earth to judge Mutabilitie's case, they assemble on "Arlo-hill"—"(Who knowes not Arlo-hill?)" (7.6.36)—the most localized earthly setting in *The Faerie Queene*. Spenser chose a setting for the trial of Mutabilitie that was practically at his back door in Ireland because he wished to emphasize the influence of Mutabilitie on the actual world in which he lived. In the hills around Kilcolman Castle, Spenser witnessed first-hand the contemporary effects of Mutabilitie's power and, specifically, the results of the "haplesse curse" which Diana lays upon the land around "Arlo-hill" (7.6.54-5). Indeed, the curse was played out in Spenser's own life when he and his family were forced to flee this troubled land. Appropriately, the *Cantos* end in personal prayer.[31]

Terrestrial Geography

"Arlo-hill" is one of the places that Spenser sets within the larger fictional earth of *The Faerie Queene*. He creates a spatial and temporal terrestrial geography around Faeryland that includes specific historical places and times, allowing him to fulfill his obligation to epic tradition by setting his poem within the known world of history. Furthermore, by coordinating this geography with his time-inclusive invented world, Spenser uses the medium of Faeryland to create epic quests that move across time. The terrestrial geography of *The Faerie Queene* includes the larger fictional earth of the poem, which Spenser usually refers to as "the world," and the local political setting of the poem in the British Isles and Western Europe, where the major historical actions originate and culminate. These last—Britain, Eden lands, Ireland, Belgium, Mercilla's Court, and Cleopolis in its political aspect—are my primary concern. But I begin with a selection of references to the larger fictional earth.

Una's parents (Adam and Eve) are of course associated with the larger world:

> [Una] by descent from Royall lynage came
> Of ancient Kings and Queenes, that had of yore
> Their scepters stretcht from East to Westerne shore,
> And all the world in their subiection held;
> Till that infernall feend with foule vprore

> Forwasted all their land, and them expeld:
> Whom to auenge, she had this Knight from far compeld.
>
> (1.1.5)

The knight is Redcrosse, who is on his way through Faeryland with Una to confront the "infernall feend" in Eden lands. As for Una's parents, trapped in their castle (1.11.3), their loss was Duessa's father's gain. Duessa tells a hopelessly wayward Redcrosse her lineage, and for once she is telling the truth: her father is a powerful "Emperour, / He that the wide West vnder his rule has, / And high hath set his throne, where *Tiberis* doth pas" (1.2.22). He represents, at once, a conqueror in the poetic fiction who defeats the king of Eden lands and wrests from him the "wide West," the "infernall feend" who triumphed over Adam, and the Roman Church, which pre-empted its papal authority from the true authority of the Universal Church.[32] The same fallen world here viewed from a Christian perspective has its classical counterpart in the world Astraea leaves when it "with sinne gan to abound" (5.1.11); she leaves Artegall to deal harsh justice in a harsh world.

The House of Holiness, where Una takes Redcrosse to have him readied for the culmination of his quest, is "Renowmd throughout the world for sacred lore" (1.10.3), and Caelia knows well that Una has "wandred through the world now long a day" (1.10.9) seeking aid for her parents. Caelia's house, like other allegorical cores, exists at the ontological and spatial limits of Faeryland: it boasts the Mount of Contemplation in its environs, and Una and Redcrosse seem to move directly from the House of Holiness to Eden lands without going back into Faeryland (see 1.10.68-1.11.2).

Una is not the only one in the poem who wanders the world. When Arthur enters the narrative, he has been seeking "fairest *Tanaquill* . . . through the world" (1.Proem.2) for "Nine monethes" (1.9.15). Artegall, Arthur's half-brother, either has a natural inclination for wandering or is forced by his work as dispenser of justice to remedy injustices throughout the world. Wherever he is when Astraea leaves him, he does not remain there. As Redcrosse tells Britomart, Artegall "ne wonneth in one certaine stead, / But restlesse walketh all the world around" (3.2.14). Before they go to Merlin to find out Artegall's whereabouts, Britomart and Glauce are ready to seek him "though beyond the *Africk Ismaell*, / Or th'Indian *Peru* he were" (3.3.6). Apparently, Satyrane shares Artegall's wandering spirit. Brought up "in forrest wyld" (1.6.21), he leaves his native land in his "ryper yeares" because he "Desird of forreine foemen to be knowne, / And far abroad for straunge aduentures sought" (1.6.29). By the time he enters the narrative, he has "fild far *landes* with glorie of his might" (1.6.20; italics added).

Spenser uses the word *land* almost as often to designate a political unit distinct from Faeryland as he does to name the solid earth.[33] The places referred to are many: lands out of history and classical mythology, Eden lands, Britain, and Ireland, among others. For example, after Britomart leaves the Temple of Isis (an allegorical core), she "Ne rested till she came without relent / Vnto the land of Amazons, as she was bent" (5.7.24). Here she defeats Radigund and frees Artegall from bondage. Spenser is not as explicit in distinguishing the land of the Amazons from Faeryland as he is in other cases, but it makes a good test case for just that reason. All the evidence points to its being distinct from Faeryland. Radigund is "Queene of Amazons" (5.4.33), and she dwells in a city: Gloriana is the only queen of Faeryland and Cleopolis its only city.[34] Radigund's land is a "common weale" (5.7.42), a political unit distinct from Faeryland; her city is a seat of political authority, a fitting place for Britomart to assume her role as Isis by restoring "true Iustice" (5.7.42). It is also fitting that Britomart and Artegall part in this political atmosphere where duty rules desire. From here Artegall enters the most dominantly political section of the poem, and he does not return to Faeryland until the end of Canto 12. He leaves Britomart in the newly reformed land of Amazons:

> There she continu'd for a certaine space,
> Til through his want her woe did more increase:
> Then hoping that the change of aire and place
> Would change her paine, and sorrow somewhat ease,
> She parted thence, her anguish to appease.
>
> (5.7.45)

Britomart perhaps returns to Faeryland, but she does not appear again in the poem.

As in the case of Radigund, "Queene of Amazons," Spenser consistently uses references to kings and queens to define distinct realms. Una and her parents are obvious examples, but there are others. (Not surprisingly, references to queens predominate except in the chronicle materials.) Hera, mentioned in passing, is "Queene of heauen," ruler of the realm from which Venus descends to earth (1.5.35); Proserpina, "Queene of hell," rules the other cosmic extreme (1.4.11). Even Duessa, who stands before Mercilla a "now vntitled Queene" (5.9.42), seems to have some formal right to the title, for she claims to be the "forsaken heire / Of that great Emperour of all the West" (1.12.26), which associates her both with the lands dominated by the Roman Church and with part of the land formerly under the control of Una's parents, telling associations when she stands before Mercilla as Mary

Queen of Scots. There are minor queens such as "*Angela*, the Saxon Queene," whose armor Britomart wears (3.3.58), and Tristram's mother, a "widow Queene" of Cornwall (6.2.29). No queen rules in Faeryland except Gloriana. Alma is "like a virgin Queene" but not a queen herself (2.11.2); and Lucifera "made her selfe a Queene," and a deluded Redcrosse even believes her, but she has no "rightfull kingdome" or "natiue soueraintie" (1.4.12).

Local Political Geography: The British Isles and Western Europe

Spenser builds a specific political geography around Faeryland, and he provides a place for Faeryland itself within this geography. Charles Bowie Millican points out the geographical distinction between Faeryland and the place where Arthur has his vision of the "Queene of Faeries" (1.9.14-5). Arthur is in northern Wales: "There, in the poet's alembic, Gloriana, England's Tudor Faery Queen, . . . found the Briton prince asleep and wooed him back to the Faeryland which was Elizabethan England." Millican identifies the boundary between Faeryland and Wales with the traditional boundary of Wales, the river Severn.[35] Ronald Arthur Horton fills out the spatial extent of Faeryland: Faeryland is Elizabethan England, "bounded in the Elizabethan imagination by the Tamar, the Severn, and the Tweed."[36] The rest of the political geography falls into place: to the north of Faeryland is Picteland (see 6.12.4); a day's journey across the sea to the west is the embattled land of "fayre *Irena*," where Artegall goes (5.12.4,10); across the sea to the south-east is the equally devastated land of "faire Belge," where Arthur goes (5.12.2,10.18); and to the southwest are the regions that Spenser names Britain—Wales and Cornwall.

All of the Briton characters—Arthur, Artegall, Britomart, and Tristram—enter Faeryland from the place that Spenser calls Britain. Arthur enters from North Wales, where he was brought up "Vnder the foot of *Rauran*" by the river Dee (1.11.4). Since the river Dee was an ancient boundary between Wales and England, it becomes in the poem a boundary between Britain and Faeryland;[37] furthermore, as A.C. Hamilton notes, "Arthur's upbringing is associated with Wales, rather than Cornwall, to link him with the ancestral home of the Tudors."[38] Artegall is linked with Cornwall through Gorlois, Duke of Cornwall, his father, and it is apparently from here that he is stolen by "false *Faries*," who bring him to Faeryland (3.3.26-7). Britomart comes to Faeryland directly from "*Deheubarth* that now South-Wales is hight," the land of her father King Ryence (3.2.18). Tristram, son of "good king *Meliogras*" of Cornwall, is sent to Faeryland from "fertile *Lionesse*" (6.2.28-30). Tristram's native land may be either the fabled land west of Cornwall between Land's End and the Scillies or the Isle of Man.[39] Redcrosse, the only Saxon hero in the poem, comes from an undisclosed location "in *Britane* land," where his ancestors "High reard their royall throne" (1.10.65).

Temporal Geography

The temporal landscape of *The Faerie Queene*, relatively straightforward outside Faeryland, becomes slippery at best within Faeryland, which I call time-inclusive, though transhistorical might also serve. The time in Britain is the sixth century (except in the case of Redcrosse), and Spenser makes the Briton characters historical contemporaries; the time in the Low Countries, France, and Ireland (except in the *Cantos of Mutabilitie*) is the sixteenth century; and specific historical references tie Mercilla's court and Cleopolis to the sixteenth century as well. Michael Murrin, who relates temporal references exclusively to Faeryland rather than to distinct places outside Faeryland, suggests that the "poet could . . . imitate. . . . a divine perspective on human history, where all the happenings in time are simultaneously present and can be seen to manifest an ordered pattern."[40] Murrin mentions four historical periods existent in *The Faerie Queene*: biblical times, the fourth century (St. George executed c. 303), the sixth century, and the Elizabethan period. He might have added a Golden Age, an age of classical myth, and a prophetic future.

Various historical times exist separately outside Faeryland and are simultaneously present within it, for Faeryland is a medium that accepts, includes, and merges times. Since Faeryland is time-inclusive, it allows historical personages from various times to exist simultaneously in Spenser's fiction. Likewise, since Faeryland is transhistorical, it allows characters and events to move across history, as all the Briton characters do. The radical example is Artegall: after being stolen out of his "infant cradle" by "false *Faries*" in sixth century Britain (3.3.26), he is lured away from "his peres" by Astraea and brought up "during Saturnes ancient raigne" (5.1.6; 5.Proem.9). When he enters the narrative in Faeryland, he enters as a contemporary of Guyon and Calidore as well as of Arthur and Britomart. It is not quite accurate to say, as Hankins does, that "Artegall lives in two centuries, the sixth and the sixteenth, in one as an actual personage of history, in the other as a reincarnation after a lapse of a thousand years,"[41] for there is no lapse of time in his career. He does not leave Britain a citizen of the sixth century to assume reincarnated form during his sojourn in Faeryland. Rather, when he enters Faeryland, he crosses over into a world capable of loosening ordinary chronology; he can be brought up in the Golden Age, fight with the Order of Maidenhead in Faeryland, and go to Ireland as Lord Gray, while remaining all the time a Briton knight, future husband of Britomart and destined king of sixth-century Britain.

Most critics who examine the temporal dimensions of *The Faerie Queene* limit Spenser's multiform anatomy of history. Roche, for example, is very specific: "the time is Uther's reign; the action is in Faeryland."[42] He, like many others, assumes that all the action takes place in Faeryland and, therefore, that no distinctions exist between the temporal characteristics of Britain and of Faeryland. Rathborne's Elysium analogue for Faeryland, combined with her recognition of a distinct setting in Britain, allows an approach to the temporal domain of the poem more complete than most. She argues, convincingly, that the poet historical would be unlikely to set the major action of his epic in a world that lacks a temporal dimension. Consequently, she sees Faeryland not as timeless but as relatively time-inclusive. Since, according to her analogue, Faeryland is a "land of the dead," it may also be identified with "the world of history," which gives meaning to all time. Faeryland includes past history because it is a land in which "departed heroes" from various times "enjoy an extended, if not an immortal life."[43] These famous dead represent the Faery population of the poem, "the race of gods and heroes who in their earthly lives anticipated the fame of Arthur and the future worthies who were destined to revive it." The "future worthies," according to Rathborne, include sixteenth-century figures present in Faeryland as "souls unborn," while the sixth-century Britons are living human beings who, like their classical counterparts, visit the land of the dead preparatory to the accomplishment of their earthly missions. Thus, Rathborne concludes, "the *Faerie Queene*, like the *Divine Comedy*, is a literary descendant of the Sixth Book of the *Aeneid*."[44]

Rathborne claims that *The Faerie Queene* includes two temporal domains: time inside Faeryland is a mythic historical time that includes the heroic past and future; time outside Faeryland, the historical present in which the poem unfolds, is the time of Uther, Arthur, Artegall, and Britomart—"sixth-century Britain." The Briton Knights "belong not to the past or to the future, like the fairies, but to the present"; "the Prince Arthur of Spenser's historical fiction passes from sixth-century Britain into the world of past history."[45] Rathborne correctly identifies Britain as spatially and temporally distinct from Faeryland, but she fails to notice other distinct historical places outside Faeryland, such as Eden lands and sixteenth-century Ireland. She also rightly observes that Spenser provides his poem with a traditional epic setting in antiquity, "furthest from the daunger of enuy, and suspition of present time," he says in the Letter to Ralegh. The sixth-century setting, however, is only one of several specific temporal domains outside Faeryland, and multiple historical references coexist in Faeryland, where past, present, and future must be treated as relative, not absolute, terms.

When Rathborne suggests that Faeryland includes past and future history, she ignores Spenser's careful discriminations among at least three narrative presents—a mythic present, a sixth-century present, and a sixteenth-century present. Spenser tends to organize references to past history in relation to the sixteenth century, not the sixth. For example, in the Proem to Book 5, Spenser explores the relationship between the golden age of "*Saturnes* ancient raigne" (9) and the "state of present time" (1). He celebrates the time when "all the world with goodnesse did abound" (9) and bemoans the deteriorated condition of "present dayes," in which "the world is runne quite out of square" and "become a stonie one" (3,1,2; see also 4.8.30-3). In this context Spenser compares "with state of present time, / The image of the antique world" (1): he contrasts the actual condition of the contemporary world, apparently present in Faeryland, with an imaginative representation of an "antique world" that appears here to represent the Golden Age, though Spenser depicts "Saturnes ancient raigne" rather loosely (see 5.1.5-12); elsewhere, the "antique world" appears to represent a legendary sixth-century historical reference also present in Faeryland as an active heroic code. The narrative setting in Faeryland is contemporary, but the ethical code by which actions in Faeryland must be judged derives from the Golden Age and may be consistent with a sixth-century heroic code. Spenser uses the word *antique* ambiguously and variously.

> Let none then blame me, if in discipline
> Of vertue and of ciuill vses lore,
> I doe not forme them of the common line
> Of present dayes, which are corrupted sore,
> But to the antique vse, which was of yore,
> When good was onely for it selfe desyred,
> And all men sought their owne, and none no more;
> When Iustice was not for the most meed outhyred,
> But simple Truth did rayne, and was of all admyred.
>
> (5.Proem.3)

Spenser supplies a supplementary set of historical references in the Proem to Book 2. The narrative present in Faeryland is still identified with the sixteenth century, for Spenser tells Elizabeth that she may behold in the "faire mirrhour" of his poem her "owne realmes in lond of Faery" (4). But he alters his reference to past history by employing a different connotation of the word *antique*: it refers not to the mythic past of the Golden Age but to the historical past of British history. Spenser calls his poem "this famous antique history" (2.Proem.1) and informs Elizabeth that she may observe "in this antique Image thy great auncestry" (4). By "famous antique history" Spenser means, literally, "well-known old story" and refers to the "historye of king Arthure" that he outlines as the core of his invention in the Letter to Ralegh. Likewise, the "antique Image" in which Elizabeth may read her genealogy refers not to the "image of the antique world" of the Proem to Book 5 (1) but to the chronicles of Britain and Faeryland that Arthur and Guyon read at Alma's castle (2.10).[46]

In the Proem to Book 2, Spenser employs the word *antique* to refer to the heroic age of ancient British history, which exists in Faeryland along with mythic and contemporary history. He also augments the perfect ethical code of the golden age with a heroic code better suited to a fallen condition. Artegall's education by Astraea is a case in point. Astraea teaches Artegall "the discipline of iustice" (5.1.6) during the Golden Age: "There she him taught to weigh both right and wrong / In equall ballance with due recompence, / And equitie to measure out along" (5.1.7). Later, when Artegall's education is complete and "the world with sinne gan to abound" (5.1.11), Astraea returns to her home in the heavens. Knowing that Artegall is destined to deal harsh justice "Mongst wicked men," she leaves her "yron man" (5.1.11,12) Talus to assist him, thus supplementing Artegall's perfect ethical code of justice derived from the golden age with a physical force commensurate with the demands of the fallen world. Similarly, Spenser creates a code of virtuous behavior consistent with history and the "termes of mortall state" by supplementing the ethical precepts of the golden age with a heroic and martial aspect.

The scene at the beginning of Book 3 illustrates both the limitations and the potential of this heroic code. In an apparently random clash of knights in the forest, Britomart unhorses Guyon, sending him to the ground behind his horse, where he nurses his wounded pride and feeds his "angry courage" (1.11). The episode depicts, humorously, the serious problem of misdirected force that attends heroic endeavors in a world of deception and evil. The scene also illustrates the positive potential of the heroic code, for after Guyon is "fairly pacifyde" by Arthur and the Palmer, the heroes enact a rite of reconciliation that binds them "with that golden chaine of concord" (3.1.11,12). At this point the narrator intrudes:

> O goodly vsage of those antique times,
> In which the sword was seruant vnto right;
> When not for malice and contentious crimes,
> But all for praise, and proofe of manly might,
> The martiall brood accustomed to fight:
> Then honour was the meed of victorie,
> And yet the vanquished had no despight:
> Let later age that noble vse enuie,
> Vile rancour to auoid, and cruell surquedrie.
>
> (3.1.13)

In this case, "antique times" refers not to the Golden Age, since that was a time when "No warre was knowne, no dreadfull trompets sound" (5.Proem.9), but to the heroic sixth century, which is at once a specific time in the past—the historical period of the Briton knights—and a narrative present in Faeryland. The "later age" refers to the sixteenth century and to the time of any reader, which are also narrative presents in Faeryland. Faeryland is, as Spenser says, a "faire mirrhour" which reflects Elizabethan England, but since the "faire mirrhour" is an allegorical fiction, its image pictures universal history. Spenser sets his epic in a multiform world of history by creating a pattern of temporal references that coexist in Faeryland and exist separately outside Faeryland.

Eden lands, Cleopolis, and Mercilla's Court

Eden lands, Mercilla's court, and Cleopolis, like Britain, embody transparent representations of history; unlike Britain, they are broadly and deeply allegorical. Eden, Una's "natiue soyle . . . where all our perils dwell," is at once the "forwasted kingdome" (1.11.2,1) that her parents rule (or ought to rule), the native land of a character who lives and breathes in the poem, the place where our perils have dwelt and dwell still, the good and the evil potential of history, and a prophetic vision of the future. It is both a particular fictional country with its own history, political structure, and populace and an allegorical representation of biblical history and the English Reformation. Eden is neither equivalent to Faeryland nor part of it, but Spenser builds Eden into the larger world of his poem by creating a political boundary between it and Faeryland. Una travels to Faeryland seeking one of its "doughtie knights" to follow her back to her own land, defend her, and rescue her parents (1.7.46). Archimago waits until he is sure that Redcrosse is "departed out of *Eden* lands" (2.1.1) before working his subtle magic to free himself. He quickly returns to Faeryland to cause more trouble. Redcrosse is on his way back to Cleopolis; but, like everyone else in the poem who once leaves that fair city, he is delayed in Faeryland proper.

Una's parents are fictional characters who rule a country outside Faeryland, but they are also Adam and Eve, whose existence is a matter of historical fact and whose story defines human history. Hence, MacCaffrey identifies Eden with "the spatio-temporal universe where human history unfolds"; she describes Redcrosse coming out of Eden and thus moving "across the boundaries between the globe of Earth and Gloriana's kingdom."[47] Eden also transcends history, for, as Frye states, "Eden is within the order of nature but it is a new earth turned upward, or sacramentally aligned with a new heaven."[48]

Spenser emphasizes Eden's dual references—to the new earth and to socio-political reality—by juxtaposing two contrasting scenes. In one, the Redcrosse knight, who is also "Saint *George* of mery England" (1.10.61) and Christ the Redeemer, fights and kills a dragon that is an agent of Duessa's father, a symbol of papal oppression, and Satan of Christian history. In the other scene, one of the most representational depictions of ordinary reality in the poem, Spenser describes the reactions of the common people to the enormous carcass of the beast:

And after, all the raskall many ran,
    Heaped together in rude rablement,
    To see the face of that victorious man:
    Whom all admired, as from heauen sent,
    And gazd vpon with gaping wonderment.
    But when they came, where that dead Dragon lay,
    Stretcht on the ground in monstrous large extent,
    The sight with idle feare did them dismay,
Ne durst approch him nigh, to touch or once assay.

Some feard, and fled; some feard and well it faynd;
    One that would wiser seeme, then all the rest,
    Warnd him not touch, for yet perhaps remaynd
    Some lingering life within his hollow brest,
    Or in his wombe might lurke some hidden nest
    Of many Dragonets, his fruitfull seed;
    Another said, that in his eyes did rest

Yet sparckling fire, and bad thereof take heed;
Another said, he saw him moue his eyes indeed.

One mother, when as her foolehardie chyld
Did come too neare, and with his talants play,
Halfe dead through feare, her little babe reuyld,
And to her gossips gan in counsell say;
How can I tell, but that his talants may
Yet scratch my sonne, or rend his tender hand?
So diuersely themselves in vaine they fray;
Whiles some more bold, to measure him nigh stand,
To proue how many acres he did spread of land.

(1.12.9-11)

Insofar as the people confront the literal monster of Spenser's fiction, their "idle feare" is justifiable, though naive; but for the reader, aware that the dragon is also Satan whom Christ has destroyed, the scene becomes humorous and the people's reactions ironic. They fear the revitalization of a demonic force that has been destroyed for all time, and those bold souls who measure how many acres the carcass covers attempt to measure the spatial extent of an idea. Spenser's conception of Eden is defined by a conscious juxtaposition of complex historical-religious allegory with a representational depiction of everyday social reality.

Cleopolis and Mercilla's court, like Eden, represent both heightened ontological states and places in the world of history. Cleopolis is, simultaneously, the ideal earthly city (see 1.10.58-9), Troynovant, London, the sovereign seat of Faeryland, and the destined setting for the realization of the Tudor apocalypse. Mercilla's court represents an ideal earthly court of law, an aspect of Cleopolis, an actual place whose architectural resemblances to Parliament and Hampton Court have been noted by critics,[49] and a distinct fictional place in the world of the poem. Gloriana and Mercilla are mighty queens, chaste and fair, who represent the ideal of just sovereignty, and they are rulers engaged in the difficult business of political government within the fallen world. They are parallel figures, representing similar ideals of queenly rule and, along with Belphoebe and Britomart, among others, aspects of Spenser's composite picture of Elizabeth. Belphoebe reflects Elizabeth's "rare chastitee," Gloriana "her rule" (3.Proem.5), and Mercilla the justice of her rule.

Obviously, Cleopolis cannot be politically distinct from Faeryland since it is that strange country's capital and only city. However, it is distanced from Faeryland like the allegorical cores and, like other historical places, "maintained as an English reality on the periphery of the poem."[50] The case of Mercilla's court is analogous; Spenser deliberately distances it from Faeryland. Dunseath suggests that as Arthur and Artegall move toward Mercilla's court, they gradually retreat "from Faeryland proper . . . to Mercilla's world of the concrete abstract—to a personified theory of justice."[51] They move, by degrees, through Mercilla's land and into her court; finally, they approach the "mayden Queene," whose "great powre and maiestie" is "Famous through all the world" (5.8.17,16).

The land ruled by Mercilla acts an an imaginative bridge between Faeryland and Elizabethan politics; Arthur and Artegall are in Mercilla's land when they save Samient, fight each other by mistake, and make peace in the beginning of Canto 8 of Book 5. The activity here seems indistinguishable from that of Faeryland, but it is in this land, not Faeryland, that Spenser chooses to portray the defeat of the Spanish Armada (5.8.28-45). At Mercilla's court, Arthur and Artegall take part in a transparent allegory of Mary Stuart's trial (5.9.38-50), and when they leave the court, they move directly into the world of Elizabethan politics. Arthur goes to Belgium as Mercilla's champion (5.10.25-26), and Artegall goes to Ireland (5.12.4) by way of France (5.11.44-65). Spenser tactfully decides to have the most transparent political allegory in *The Faerie Queene* proceed from a place representing ideal Elizabethan justice. Moreover, his portrayal of Mercilla's court and of the action that proceeds from it is yet another instance of his conscious distancing of actual political events from his imagined world.

3. Faeryland and the Larger World

Thomas Roche's approach to the world of *The Faerie Queene* exemplifies traditional critical assumptions concerning the setting of Spenser's poem: "*The Faerie Queene* is different from all other epics in that it exists in a world entirely of Spenser's creation. Homer, Virgil, Ariosto, and Tasso, whether they wrote of the mythical or historical past, 'set' their epics in a known world, at least a world with recognizable dimensions and locations."[52] Roche is partially correct: unlike other epic poets in the classical line, including Dante and Milton, Spenser sets most of the action of his poem in an invented world. However, as I have shown, Spenser does set his epic within a known world, and he coordinates specific places and times outside Faeryland with spatial and temporal references inside his imagined world to create a complex and consistent anatomy of history.

Murrin makes essentially the same point as Roche, but he states it in relation to romance rather than epic: "In other romances fairyland is a place visited amidst a number of adventures set in more mundane lands. . . . Spenser alone staged all his action there, in the land where all other romances cross over, one into another."[53] This assertion would be accurate if Murrin had written "most of his action" rather than "all his action," for unlike most other writers of romances, Spenser makes his imagined world the dominant setting of his poem. But Faeryland is neither the only setting in *The Faerie Queene* nor the kind of setting that Murrin goes on to describe: "Images and personifications [in Faeryland] appear and disappear in a largely deserted landscape. This dreamy sense contrasts markedly with the Italian romantic epic. Tasso and Ariosto both present coherent societies with a real geography and history."[54] Murrin seems to employ the word *dreamy* in the manner that Lewis warns against, for his use of the word suggests "the dimness and evasiveness" of "waking reverie" rather than the "violent clarity and precision" of "actual dreams."[55] Furthermore, Murrin argues that life in Faeryland, as in dreams, "systematically violates our notions of probability"; in short, he asserts that Spenser does not "create a probable and real world."[56]

My dual aim in this chapter has been to explore the ways in which Spenser does create a "probable and real world" in Faeryland and to show how he situates his imagined world within a larger fictional world of "real geography and history." Even if I were to admit that Spenser fails to "present coherent societies" in Faeryland, I would argue that these societies exist in the socio-political settings outside Faeryland. Cleopolis, Mercilla's court, and Eden lands are not "mundane" in the same way as the primary settings in romances to which Murrin alludes; however, Spenser does create a setting outside Faeryland that corresponds at once to the "mundane lands" out of which romance heroes emerge and to the traditional representational setting of heroic epic. This place is the Britain of *The Faerie Queene*, to which I now turn.

Notes
Chapter III

1. MacCaffrey, *Spenser's Allegory*, 67.

2. Robert Scholes and Robert Kellogg, *The Nature of Narrative* (New York: Oxford Univ. Press, 1966), 82.

3. John B. Bender, *Spenser and Literary Pictorialism* (Princeton: Princeton Univ. Press, 1972), 66.

4. This is no place for an essay on the general "idealizing" tendency among critics who describe the world of *The Faerie Queene*. Suffice it to say that the tendency to examine Faeryland as a representation of ideal, unfallen, or "romantic" existence in a golden world of wish fulfillment and human perfection is manifest throughout Spenserian studies. Faeryland *is* distanced from everyday experience, but it and the larger fictional world Spenser builds around it are, as Spenser would say, mirrors reflecting reality from a number of perspectives. Critics who tend to be exclusive in their definitions of Faeryland, who limit the world of the poem, are not wrong: their descriptions are merely incomplete. As for recent historicist critics, theirs is the same problem in different guise. This book is an amendment to the dominant tendency.

5. Rathborne, *Meaning*, 144, 157.

6. Rathborne, 145, 201.

7. Rathborne, 153.

8. Rathborne, 143, 149.

9. C.S. Lewis's pioneering *Allegory of Love* (1936) has influenced much subsequent Spenserian scholarship in one way or another. Lewis's approach to the allegory of *The Faerie Queene* has been especially influential. An example will better serve than a paraphrase of theory to summarize Lewis's approach. In showing how Guillaume de Lorris is "more of a realist than Chrétien," Lewis insists that we not be "deceived by the allegorical form." The use of allegory "does not mean that the author is talking about non-entities, but that he is talking about the inner world—talking, in fact, about the realities he knows best. No doubt, from a grammatical or logical point of view, the land of Gorre in *Lancelot* is 'concrete,' and Danger in the *Roman*, being a personification, is 'abstract.' But no one, least of all Chrétien, has ever been to the land of Gorre, while Guillaume, or any courtly lover of the period—or, for that matter, any lover in any subsequent period—has actually met Danger. In other words, the 'concrete' places and people in Chrétien are mere romantic supposals: the 'abstract' places and people in the *Ro-*

mance of the Rose are presentations of actual life" (115). I would argue that Spenser is both an "abstract" realist like Guillaume and a "concrete" realist like Chrétien but that Faeryland is not a "romantic supposal."

Compare Kathleen Williams, *Spenser's World of Glass: A Reading of* The Faerie Queene (Berkeley: Univ. of California Press, 1966), xiii-xv, 16; Northrop Frye, *A Study of English Romanticism* (New York: Random House, 1968), 130; Hayden Carruth, "Spenser and His Modern Critics," *Hudson Review* 22 (1969):140; MacCaffrey, *Spenser's Allegory*, 71.

10. Harry Berger, Jr., Introduction to *Spenser: A Collection of Critical Essays*, ed. Berger (Englewood Cliffs, NJ: Prentice-Hall, 1968), 4. In his article "The Renaissance Imagination: Second World and Green World," *Centennial Review* 9 (1965): 47, Berger presents some specific examples of the "second world": "More's Utopia, Sidney's golden world and Arcadia, Spenser's Faerie, Shakespeare's green world and stage world, Marvell's poetic gardens, Alberti's picture plane as a window, Leonardo's painted second nature, Filarte's Sforzinda, Castiglione's Urbino, Machiavelli's hypothetical state, Gilbert's magnetic terrella, Galileo's experiment world, and the new world described in Descartes' *Discourse*."

11. Berger, "The Renaissance Imagination," 49. (Berger recognizes and approves Meyer Abrams'use of the term *heterocosm*.) He argues that "Frye does not clearly distinguish the actual normal world from the fictional 'world represented as a normal world,' the actual red and white world of history from its image in fiction. There is a difference between the second world *in* a fiction and the second world *as* a fiction" (48, italics Berger's). Since the heterocosmic fiction may include more than one fictional world, it allows "the clarity and simplicity of the green world [to] be balanced by the variety of an imaginary field in which a number of such worlds coexist" (49). Compare Northrop Frye, "The Structure of Imagery in *The Faerie Queene*," *University of Toronto Quarterly* 30 (1960-1): 112-4; and Frye, *Anatomy of Criticism*, 158-86.

12. On Faeryland as an image of dream-reality, see Graham Hough, *A Preface to* The Faerie Queene (New York: Norton, 1962), passim, especially 96, 133-7; compare C.S. Lewis, *English Literature in the Sixteenth Century, Excluding Drama* (1954; rpt. Oxford: Clarendon Press, 1968), 387.

13. Lewis, *Allegory of Love*, 113-5, explains that it is the nature of allegory to paint the "inner world." And MacCaffrey (179) offers a corrective to those critics who allow this approach to restrict their interpretations: "An awareness of the various kinds of reality which Spenser understood to be the referents of his images must prevent us from saying that all the events of *The Faerie Queene* take place exclusively 'in the mind' of one or another character."

14. MacCaffrey, 74.

15. Foster Provost, "Treatments of Theme and Allegory in Twentieth-Century Criticism of *The Faerie Queene,*" in *Contemporary Thought on Edmund Spenser*, ed. Richard C. Frushell and Bernard J. Vondersmith (Carbondale, IL: Southern Illinois Univ. Press, 1975), 32, summarizes some of the elements of Spenser's fiction that coalesce in what he calls a "permanently ambiguous matrix from which the poet derives the visionary land of his poem": "England under the historical aspect; the transitory, deceptive phenomenal world which we all experience; a symbolic landscape which represents the interior experiences of the human psyche in the struggle of existence; and a 'golden world' peopled by denizens more perfected, nearer the ideal than can be found in our experience." Pauline Parker (54-5) names the levels of experience in Faeryland the literal, the historical, and the spiritual; Hough (134) names them "the romantic, the historical, the moral, and the psychological"; and Murrin, *Allegorical Epic* (144), the literal, psychological, philosophical, and theological.

16. Lewis, *Allegory of Love*, 334; see also 334-46. Durling, *Figure*, 269n, provides a clear summary of Spenser's multiple use of allegory:

> The referent of the allegory can be single or multiple at different times and can shift radically. It is thus possible for Spenser to have the best of both worlds: if the story is for the most part an intermittent metaphor whose referent is true, there are also occasions when it must be understood as literally true in the historical sense (such as much of the chronicles in II.10). . . . On a further level of abstraction, Spenser will give a translation of actual events into an allegorical scheme which reveals their inner nature without changing their identity (the story of Burbon is a good example). On the most abstract level, the allegorical scheme represents the general principle of which any given historical event is an individual, partial embodiment (thus the trial of Duessa, V.10, is primarily an analysis of the relation between mercy and justice in the abstract; the trial of Mary of Scotland is a secondary referent).

See also Frank Kermode, *Shakespeare, Spenser, Donne* (New York: Viking 1971), 60; MacCaffrey, 111; Pauline Parker, 13, 27-65.

17. Scholes and Kellogg, *Nature of Narrative*, 93.

18. Rosemond Tuve, *Allegorical Imagery: Some Medieval Books and Their Posterity* (Princeton:Princeton Univ. Press, 1966), 390-2; see also 378-80.

19. MacCaffrey, 61-4. She cites Edgar Wind, *Pagan Mysteries in the Renaissance* (rev. ed., Harmondsworth, Mx., 1967), 206, as her source for the terms "unfolded" and "infolded". In general, MacCaffrey treats Spenser's allegory as extended metaphor; she does not use I.A. Richards' terms "tenor" and "vehicle," but she makes the same point I do when she discusses "different versions of metaphor."

20. MacCaffrey, 94.

21. MacCaffrey, 62-4. She cites Angus Fletcher, *Allegory: The Theory of a Symbolic Mode* (Ithaca, NY: Cornell Univ. Press, 1964), 321, whose distinction between "allegory" and "myth" is analogous to the one she draws between "analytic" and "synthetic" allegory.

22. Mammon dwells in a great cavern inside the gates of Hell (2.7.25-6,28) but not, apparently, in Hades proper; Guyon looks down into the river Cocytus from the Garden of Proserpina (2.7.53,56-67). Guyon and Mammon do not cross the river into Hades itself.

MacCaffrey (143) argues that the Cave of Night and the Mount of Contemplation are the "poles [of the] axis of . . . pseudo-visionary reality" in Book 1. However, she does not point out that while the Cave, which Duessa visits on "the easterne coast of heauen" (1.5.19), is outside Faeryland, the Mount probably exists at the upper ontological limit of Faeryland.

23. Harry Berger, Jr., "The *Mutabilitie Cantos*: Archaism and Evolution in Retrospect," in *Spenser: A Collection of Critical Essays*, ed. Berger (Englewood Cliffs, NJ: Prentice-Hall, 1968), 150.

24. Frye, *Study of Romanticism*, 104. In "The Structure of Imagery," 112-4, during a discussion of the *Mutabilitie Cantos*, Frye provides a more thorough outline of the four cosmic levels: (1) "the level of death, corruption, and dissolution"; (2) "the world of ordinary experience," including "becoming or change" plus "a principle of order or recurrence within which the change occurs" (from "the perspective of Faerie," this realm is divided into "a human moral world and a demonic one"); (3) "upper nature, the stars and their courses," a realm unchanged by the fall and ruled by Nature, "whose viceroy" is Jove; (4) "Above Nature is the real God" and the Christian heaven.

25. MacCaffrey, 185.

26. MacCaffrey, 94.

27. MacCaffrey, 267.

28. Harry Berger, Jr., "Spenser's Gardens of Adonis: Force and Form in the Renaissance Imagination," *University of Toronto Quarterly* 30 (1960-61): 136.

29. Berger, "*Mutabilitie Cantos*," 150.

30. Lewis, *Allegory of Love*, 354.

31. Spenser usually distinguishes places associated with the gods of classical myth from Faeryland proper. For instance, Proteus' den, where Florimell is imprisoned and where the mythological marriage of the Thames and Medway takes place, is explicitly distinguished from Faeryland: when Marinell frees Florimell "from *Proteus* cruell band," he takes her directly back "againe to Faerie land" (5.3.2). There is at least one obvious reason why Proteus' den is not located in Faeryland: it is far out at sea and clearly not within an inland sea like Phaedria's island or the Bower of Bliss. But there are possible reasons for Spenser's distinction other than simple geography. First, Proteus is a god, even if a minor one, and I have noted the problematical relationship of immortal beings to Faeryland. Second, Proteus' den is the setting for the great marriage that closes Book 4, a mythological marriage that unites beings representing two actual rivers and is attended by the spirits of other rivers, especially ones from England and Ireland. This seems to be another case in which Spenser keeps transparent representations of actual places outside Faeryland. Only the names are real in this case, but the spirits come from actual geographical locations, and perhaps this fact was enough to make Spenser place them outside Faeryland.

32. See Hamilton, ed., *The Faerie Queene*, annotations to 1.1.5 and 1.2.22-4; Kermode, *Shakespeare, Spenser, Donne*, 42-3.

33. See Charles Grosvenor Osgood, *A Concordance to the Poems of Edmund Spenser* (The Carnegie Institution of Washington, 1915), citations under *land.*

34. Hankins, *Source and Meaning*, 55, notes: "Though the final destination of the virtuous quest is a city, Cleopolis, there is a surprising absence of cities throughout Spenser's Fairyland. Such centers of population as there are are castles or palaces or temples or cottages, but never a number of these close together. Each one seems to exist in isolation. . . . Even such royal courts as the castle of Una's parents and the palace of Mercilla do not seem to be part of a larger urban community. . . . They stand in a boundless forest which is limited only by the surrounding sea."

35. Millican, 145-6.

36. Horton, *Unity*, 31, outlines a local spatial geography for *The Faerie Queene* similar to the one I expose. Rathborne, *Meaning*, cites classical and Celtic sources (144, n. 212) that locate the "land of the dead" on "an island in the west" (181); consequently, she calls Faeryland the "fairy counterpart" of Britain (192). Michael Murrin locates Faeryland "literally as a place" "in India and finally in America" ("The Rhetoric of Faeryland," in *The Rhetoric of Renaissance Poetry*, ed. Thomas O. Sloan and Raymond B. Waddington [Berkeley: Univ. of California Press, 1974], 91, 78). As a result, he claims that "Faery is . . . a dream of empire" (*Allegorical Epic*, 139).

37. See Hamilton, ed., *The Faerie Queene*, annotation to 1.9.4.7.

38. Hamilton, ed., *The Faerie Queene*, annotation to 1.9.4.5-8.

39. Hamilton, ed., *The Faerie Queene*, annotation to 6.2.30.4, suggests the fabled land. Robert O. Evans has suggested to me that Spenser's reference may be to the Isle of Man and has pointed out an interesting relationship between the political geography and the linguistic divisions of Spenser's day. Spenser's Britain represents a Celtic area including Wales, where Welsh was spoken, and the Isle of Man and Cornwall, where two separate Celtic languages were spoken. Ireland is of course associated with the Irish language and Picteland with Highland Scots. From this perspective, we see Spenser distinguishing various language groups from the Germanic-Saxon-Anglo-Norman English of Elizabethan Faeryland, which is the vernacular language of his epic.

40. Michael Murrin, *The Veil of Allegory: Some Notes toward a Theory of Allegorical Rhetoric in the English Renaissance* (Chicago: Univ. of Chicago Press, 1969), 109-10.

41. Hankins, *Source*, 150.

42. Roche, *Flame*, 47.

43. Rathborne, *Meaning*, 151, 143, 142-3.

44. Rathborne, vii, 151,n.320, vii.

45. Rathborne, 189, 204, 189.

46. Spenser sometimes uses the word *antique* as a value term meaning better or more perfect and sometimes as a general reference to the imaginative time in which the whole poem exists. For instance, the "antique rolles" that Spenser invokes his "holy Virgin" muse to "lay forth out of [her] euerlasting scryne" (1.Proem 2) refer to the exemplary subject matter of the poem, whose temporal references are multiple and ambiguous. Compare Frye, "Structure of Imagery," 113; Horton, *Unity*, 33-6; and Thomas M. Greene, "antique world," in *Spenser Encyclopedia*, 42-6.

47. MacCaffrey, 209.

48. Frye, "Structure of Imagery," 188-9.

49. See Hamilton, ed., *The Faerie Queene*, annotation to 5.9.27.9.

50. Nohrnberg, *Analogy*, 207.

51. Dunseath, *Spenser's Allegory of Justice*, 207, see also 212.

52. Roche, *Flame*, 32.

53. Murrin, "The Rhetoric of Faeryland," 82.

54. Murrin, *Allegorical Epic*, 144.

55. Lewis, *English Literature*, 387.

56. Murrin, *Allegorical Epic*, 144, 145.

Chapter IV
Britain and the Epic Quests

1. Britain and Faeryland

The Britain of *The Faerie Queene* is the place in southwestern Great Britain from which the Briton characters enter Faeryland. Like certain other distinct fictional places, it is not ruled by Gloriana and is therefore separated from Faeryland by a political boundary; like Eden, Cleopolis, Mercilla's land, and the lands of Irena and Belge, Britain is a transparent representation of history. Spenser outlines explicitly the sixth-century historical setting in Britain. Ryence, Britomart's father, is away at war assisting Uther against the Saxons (see 3.2.18, 3.52–60). Gorlois, Duke of Cornwall, Artegall's father, is long since dead, having been slain, as Malory tells, on the same night that his wife Igrayne conceived Arthur by Uther (disguised by Merlin to resemble her husband).[1] Uther has married Igrayne, and Arthur has been, as Spenser says in the Letter to Ralegh, "by Merlin armed, and by Timon throughly instructed."[2] He has recently departed from Britain in search of the Faery Queen when Britomart and her nurse Glauce make their way through a war-torn Britain to seek Artegall in Faeryland (see 3.3.61). Tristram is soon to be sent to the relative safety of Faeryland, since his mother fears for his life at the hands of her dead husband's brother, who has usurped Tristram's rightful throne (see 6.2.28–30).

The historical setting in Britain is unique in the world of the poem, for it is the only sustained representational depiction of socio-political reality in

The Faerie Queene. As such it is related to two distinct literary settings: the traditional geographical and political world of heroic epic and the primary setting in medieval romance—often Arthur's court—away from which the heroes move on their adventures. Spenser uses Britain in conjunction with Faeryland and Cleopolis to provide a setting consistent with his combined epic and romance quests. Arthur and Britomart leave Britain in search of the ones they love, but they carry with them the epic potential of historical destiny. Britain and Cleopolis form a Virgilian epic frame around the allegorical, romance, and minor epic actions that make up the life of the poem in Faeryland. Britomart and Artegall will return to Britain, where, like Aeneas, they will begin to build a nation out of chaos; Arthur will reach Cleopolis, where, by serving and marrying Gloriana, he will initiate the prophetic nation of the Tudor apocalypse. Britain is analogous to Aeneas' Latium and Cleopolis to the prophetic Rome.

When critics examine the Britain of *The Faerie Queene*, they do not approach it as a place within a larger world; rather, since most consider Faeryland coextensive with the world of the poem, they identify Britain with various kinds of references to history within Faeryland. They find these references in the British chronicle material and its Faery counterpart and in distinctions between Briton and Faery knights or between things Briton and things Faery. As a rule, critics use these kinds of distinctions to create dualistic interpretive models analogous to those drawn from distinctions between Faeryland and the real world, second world and first world, fiction and fact; at the end of this sequence, inevitably it would seem, comes the distinction between ideal and real. As a theoretical foundation upon which to build, these dualities serve a useful purpose; but they cannot stand as sufficient models for distinctions between Britain and Faeryland any more than they can stand for distinctions between the world of the poem and the apprehendable universe. To conclude that Britain represents the real world of history is not far from accurate, but to propose that Faeryland represents an ideal world is to distort Spenser's imagined world and limit the scope of his fiction.

Since most critics treat Britain as a general historical reference of Faeryland without noting that it is also one of several references as well as one of several distinct places outside Faeryland, their discussions are often couched in ambiguous terminology. Edwin Greenlaw's 1918 article "Spenser's Fairy Mythology" provides important critical background concerning the Britain of the poem, an example of the distinction between Britain as a place and as an idea, and an occasion for noting some of the common assumptions and pitfalls, including inconsistent terminology, that characterize critical treatment of Britain.[3]

In Faeryland, Greenlaw says, "Spenser fuses the well known romance and folklore conception of a land of enchantment, difficult of access, with a quite arbitrary and literal conception of England as the scene in which the action of his poem takes place." Greenlaw makes no distinction of place here; Faeryland and England coexist as concepts in a single fictional world, "the realm of Gloriana." This realm is "two-fold: England, in the historical allegory; the Celtic Otherworld in the fairy aspect." Greenlaw's use of the term *England* is comprehensive; it names every reference to history, darkly veiled or transparent, whether it occurs in the place Spenser identifies as Faeryland or in some other locale. When Greenlaw turns to an identification of places, he employs inconsistent terminology. He identifies Faeryland with Wales and at the same time with the "literal conception of England as the scene in which the action of [the] poem takes place."[4] "By *Fairy* Spenser means *Welsh*, or, more accurately, *Tudor*, as distinguished from the general term British." But he says that Spenser "looks on England as Britain."[5] These designations ignore distinctions between events set in sixth-century Britain and those set in a contemporary English historical sphere, and they leave no place from which Briton characters may enter Faeryland, as Greenlaw knows they do. He is apparently aware of the difficulty, for he attempts to patch up his geography by using the term *Great Britain* to name the place from which the Briton knights enter Faeryland: "Britomart says that she has come from her 'natiue soyle, that is by name the greater Britaine,' to 'Faery lond.'" But he misappropriates the term, for he apparently conceives her coming out of Great Britain into Faeryland, which, "for the moment, is Wales, the last stronghold of Britain."[6] Wales is not Faeryland; Britomart's "greater Britaine" is Wales, and she enters Faeryland from "South-wales" (3.2.7,18).

As might be expected of the careful historian, Spenser always is consistent in his use of names to describe distinct historical places. He employs Britain (Britayne, Britaine) interchangeably with Britany to describe the setting for the British history of *Briton moniments* (2.10) and Merlin's prophecy to Britomart (3.3.26–50).[7] Likewise, he uses Briton to identify figures out of history whom he wishes to distinguish from Saxons or Paynims or Romans. Britain also is the name Spenser uses to indicate the Celtic region of southwestern Great Britain—Wales and Cornwall—from which the Britons enter Faeryland.

Redcrosse is the only character in the poem whom Spenser refers to as English. He is a Saxon native of "*Britane* land" (1.10.65) but "sprong out from English race," "borne of English blood" and destined to be "Saint *George* of mery England" (1.10.60,64,61), the patron saint of all the English people. Redcrosse is not involved in the political matters that tie the Briton knights to sixth-century Britain. The allegory of his quest reflects English religious history and biblical history, beside which, for a Christian poet, even political history of epic proportions must pale in significance. Spenser names Redcrosse *English* to single him out, just as he singles out "Dan *Chaucer*, well of English vndefyled" (4.2.32), using the word for proud praises of a united England, of one people speaking one language and embracing one religion.

Spenser's only other uses of the words *England* and *English* occur in references to the rivers attending the marriage of Thames and Medway, where he employs political and geographical connotations. The carefully articulated geography at the foundation of Spenser's river pageant celebrates the peaceful coexistence of England, Ireland, and Wales in a united English commonwealth. It also calls attention to the boundaries Spenser conceives between Faeryland and Britain:[8] "the speedy Tamar, which diuides / The Cornish and the Deuonish confines" and the "stately Seuerne" and "following Dee" (4.11.31, 30, 39), which form a rough, disputed boundary between England and Wales. The Dee, "which Britons long ygone / Did call diuine" (4.11.39), is of course the river near whose source Arthur says he was reared (1.9.4); it "was held to possess magical power of divination: its change of course prophesied victory to the English or the Welsh."[9] There may be some veiled political allusions in Spenser's brief description of the Severn. After the entrance of the bridegroom (Thames) and his train, "Then came his neighbour floods, which nigh him dwell, / And water all the English soile throughout" (4.11.30). The English and Welsh rivers pay homage to the Thames, as do the Irish rivers, "Sith no lesse famous then the rest they bee, / And ioyne in neighborhood of kingdome nere" (4.11.40). At the head of this train is the Severn:

> They all on [Thames] this day attended well;
> And with meet seruice waited him about;
> Ne none disdained low to him to lout:
> No not the stately Seuerne grudg'd at all.
>
> (4.11.30)

The possibility that he might have "grudg'd" seems implicit, and the fact that he and the Welsh rivers do not signifies the unification of England and Wales in the Tudor line. In addition, the river-marriage is a type of Arthur's quest, which originates in Wales and moves through Faeryland toward its culmination in Cleopolis, where the prophetic English nation would be established in Arthur's marriage to Gloriana.

I follow Spenser in using *Britain* to name the Britons' native land and to signify a historically determined idea which helps to define distinctions between the Briton and Faery knights and between the chronicles of Britain and Faeryland. Like Spenser, I use *England* to name Elizabethan England and to identify the united nation prophesied in the river-marriage. The distinctions Spenser draws between sixth-century Britain and sixteenth-century England and between the idea of Britain and the place ought to be kept in mind during the discussion that follows, for most critics ignore them, and even those few who recognize Britain as a distinct place treat the fact as insignificant and discuss Britain as, exclusively, an aspect of Faeryland. In doing so they limit the scope of Spenser's epic setting and simplify his careful structuring of the epic quests. Nonetheless, since the idea of Britain informs the place, critical commentary on the idea impinges upon my discussion of the place.

In *A Preface to* The Faerie Queene, Graham Hough outlines the three major ways that the idea of Britain enters the poem, only to discredit their usefulness as means of interpretation: "So Queen Elizabeth is furnished with two genealogies, one supposedly historic, through the British kings, and one purely in the fairy line. In the face of this it is surely impossible to distinguish clearly (as Greenlaw and others try to do) between British and fairy knights, or to see any subtle significance behind the distinction between Britain and Fairy Land. The Britain of *The Faerie Queene* is England, and so is Fairy Land."[10] But Spenser does represent actual history in the British chronicle material, he explicitly distinguishes Briton knights from Faery, and he draws direct and suggestive distinctions between Britain and Faeryland. In *The Allegorical Temper*, Harry Berger provides a rejoinder to the kinds of assertions made by Hough and others: "Too many Spenserian commentators have hindered their own operations by following an either/or strategy in this matter. Either they have felt it necessary to dissolve Faery into historical Britain, or else they have suppressed the factualities of Britain and lingered on the golden fantasies of Faery."[11] Since Berger knows that interpretations of *The Faerie Queene* that fail to recognize the importance of both "mythical Faery" and "historical Britain" tend to distort Spenser's fiction, he argues that the poem ought to be read within a framework "in which Faery must be defined by Britain and Britain by Faery": "Like two terms of a simile, Britain and Faery confront each other to produce a third entity compact of their similarities and differences. This entity is the intelligible world, the poem itself."[12] Berger's analysis of the idea of Britain has remained substantially unchallenged to this day, and critics are indebted to Berger's exploration of three related British aspects of *The Faerie Queene*: Britain as a general reference to the world of history, the British chronicle in contrast to the Faery chronicle, and Briton knights as distinct from Faery.

Thomas Roche's discussion of Britain and Faeryland serves as a good introduction to more detailed examination because it exposes some problems that Berger attempts to avoid. Although Roche is in essential agreement with Berger, his consistently idealistic approach to Faeryland as the world of the poem conditions and finally obscures the distinction he draws between Britain and Faeryland. According to Roche, "Faeryland is the ideal world of the highest, most virtuous *human* achievements." It is "outside space," "outside time," and "non-Christian." The spatial, temporal, and Christian entities are supplied by references to Britain and England (Roche makes no apparent distinction). Taken together, the ideas of Britain and Faeryland define the poem as "an ideal of civil life that is to occur historically during the reign of the Tudors."[13] Roche notes that Spenser is "concerned to maintain a complex relationship between the historical and geographical locale he may have chosen and the locale where his marvelous adventures occur." The first, "the real world of history and geography," Roche identifies with "the red and white world of Tudor history" and with "the progress and triumph of British nationalism." The second, "the green world of Faeryland," Roche finds represented in the Faery chronicle.[14] The British chronicle is "a history of an individual nation within the Providential design of Christian history," which is "fixed within the limits of Fall and Apocalypse." The Faery chronicle, on the other hand, represents "the expanding cycle of human glory," which is "always increasing, pushing hard against the consequences of that First Sin. Those who have pushed hardest and become ideals are the stuff of which Faeryland is made."[15] Roche's analysis of his distinction between the real world of English history and the ideal world of Faery history seems consistent, but it is incomplete. Since he assumes that all the action takes place in the imagined green world of Faeryland,[16] Roche allows real history to be conditioned by its existence in Faeryland. He outlines not a real and an ideal history but two ideal historical references of Faeryland: an ideal Tudor history and an ideal universal history of human glory. His approach leaves no room for the hard facts of actual sixth- and sixteenth-century political matters, which exist outside of Faeryland and which intrude into Spenser's imagined world. The whole of history may possess an ideal potential that culminates in "the triumph of the Tudor Apocalypse,"[17] but this potential is severely tested in a fictional world, ruled by the "termes of mortall state" (3.4.28), in which history is anything but ideal.[18]

Berger's analysis of distinctions between Britain and Faeryland is both more thorough and more consistent than that of many critics who follow him. The differences he recognizes between the British chronicle (*Briton moniments*) and the Faery chronicle (*Antiquitie* of *Faerie* lond) form the foundation of his approach: "The point about the two chronicles is the very clear contrast between them: they present two different worlds, two utterly irreconcilable views of life, two opposed modes of memory, perception, and consciousness. We see Arthur reading the first and Guyon the second; we see that the first expresses the very quintessence of what Arthur is and knows and does, and that it embodies a historical realism deliberately excluded from the unrealistic and mythic chronicle of *Faeryland*. The unreality of the latter—seven stanzas of excellence, peace, and power, undisturbed succession and order—is further emphasized by the fact that it follows the (sixty-four stanzas of) sweat and blood which marked the British history. Not only is it inappropriate for Guyon to read the British history; it scarcely seems possible."[19] Berger emphasizes the radical differences between the two chronicles, but he avoids labeling Faery history ideal. It lacks the "historical realism" of the British history Arthur reads, but it is "mythic" rather than ideal. His distinction suggests one that might be drawn between the political history of the chroniclers and the interest in cultural myth among some of the antiquaries.

The differences between the two chronicles are undeniable. The British chronicle material, both *Briton moniments*, which Arthur reads (2.10.4–68), and Merlin's prophecy, which Britomart hears (3.3.26–49), deserves to be called real history, despite inaccuracies and Spenserian manipulations: it comprises human names, bloodshed, and political chaos. Next to it the Faery chronicle, which Guyon reads (2.10.70–6), seems ideal, even its names distanced by fiction. But Spenser knits them together at their ends: both the Faery chronicle and Merlin's prophecy conclude with transparent references to Elizabeth and her immediate ancestors (2.10.75–6; 3.3.48–9). The knot is closely tied, for Tannaquill of the Faery chronicle, who is Gloriana, queen of Faeryland, is also the "royall virgin" Elizabeth of Merlin's prophecy, who will "Stretch her white rod ouer the *Belgicke* shore" (3.3.49), as Mercilla does in Book 5. There is no place at the end of the chronicles for categorizations such as real and ideal or even actual and fictional. If there is finally a distinction to be made, it is between the representational history of Britain and the allegorical history of Faeryland.

The distinction between Briton and Faery knights has been in the corpus of modern Spenserian studies since Greenlaw distinguished them by "race" and Rathborne in terms of living Briton and dead or unborn Faery knights.[20] Berger draws a distinction between Briton and Faery knights consistent with the one between Britain and Faeryland that he derives from the chronicle material: "Elfin and Briton symbolize two modes of existence, two basic types of human disposition, two quite different relationships holding between conscious and unconscious. . . . What is emphasized about Guyon and Gloriana is an excellence which is secure and self-sufficient because it has its roots in a special gift of nature. The excellence of Redcrosse, Arthur, and Britomart is of a different kind, for it is ultimately actualized in terms of their insufficiency: each tends in love towards an object painfully remote; each is directly moved by the knowledge of that incompleteness (though it must be forced on Redcrosse)."[21] The Briton knights are "relatively complicated, ambiguous, continually changing and developing figures whose destinies lie beyond Faerie in the historical world."[22] Driven by love and historical destiny, they use their heroic strength of character to overcome their native insufficiencies. The static excellence of the Faery (Berger's Elfin) knights, their "Aristotelian sophrosyne,"[23] allows them a self-sufficiency the Briton knights must labor to acquire. However, their native excellence, as Berger shows, is in effect a liability, for it causes self-centeredness in both Guyon and Calidore and hinders their abilities to confront the hard trials of mortal and heroic existence.[24] The native strength of the Briton knights consists of just the ability the Faery knights lack: it is their nature to confront failure, endure pain, and overcome obstacles, and this nature makes them, paradoxically, more fit for Faeryland—or anywhere else in the fallen world—than the Faeries.

Many critics have noticed differences between British and Faery books of *The Faerie Queene*, those whose heroes are, respectively, Britons and Faeries. Berger sets forth the general notion: "Books I, III, and V are primarily British books because they are, in different ways, approaches to the real or the actual—as theological, as natural, as social. But II, IV, VI seem to involve corresponding withdrawals into Faerie."[25] Ronald Horton's approach supplements Berger's: "Holiness, chastity, and justice, in Spenser's treatment, . . . consist of conformity to an absolute divine standard, whereas temperance, friendship, and courtesy consist of practical norms of behavior." The distinction is between "supernatural and intuitive" virtues on the one hand and "natural and empirical" on the other; the moral reference of the first is vertical and of the second horizontal. "Paradoxically, the intuitive virtues must be developed through a process of education by the human [Briton] knights, whereas the acquired virtues are instinctively possessed and practiced by the fairy knights."[26]

Angus Fletcher, though he agrees with Rathborne that Britons are living and Faeries dead or unborn, defines the distinction between them in a way that complements Berger's: "the interaction of the two modes of heroic existence, faery and Briton, is an interaction of two aspects of time, its recurrent forms and its linear, evolutionary forms."[27] MacCaffrey notes that Redcrosse's "vision is a token of the fact that he is 'sprong out of English race'" and, like all Britons, involved in the linear and evolutionary time of political and Christian history. The object of his vision, the heavenly Jerusalem, is the consummation of history; it "takes us out of the fiction and into the realm that fictions reflect."[28] The Britons and their quests include a historical dimension—an access to history—that the Faeries and their quests lack.

2. The Quests from Cleopolis

Thus far I have limited discussion of differences between Britain and Faeryland and Briton and Faery characters to evidence drawn from the chronicle material and interpretations of the general natures of the heroes and their books. Critics have all but ignored another source of evidence: Britons and Faeries are conditioned by their respective native lands, and their origins determine the natures of their quests. The major epic quests—those of Redcrosse, Britomart, Artegall, and Arthur—evolve within a world larger than Faeryland, and the heroes' movements between distinct places define in part the meanings of their quests. The lack of critical inquiry into this area is no surprise considering that all but a very few critics approach Faeryland as equivalent to the world of the poem. What remains surprising, however, is that even those few, such as Berger and MacCaffrey, who recognize at least that the Britons enter Faeryland from Britain or are headed from Faeryland to a place called Britain, disregard the significance of the larger setting and discuss Britain only as an aspect of Faeryland.[29] Nonetheless, everything that has already been said concerning the ideas of Britain and Faeryland forms a consistent background for what follows.

The Briton knights are traditional epic heroes, bound, like Aeneas, to historical destiny and to consequent political responsibilities;[30] they inherit a heroic energy commensurate with their obligation to confront the kind of representational historical reality depicted in the British chronicles. The Faery knights, on the other hand, are natives of Faeryland who owe allegiance solely to Gloriana in her role as queen of Faeryland. Their quests, exclusively social and ethical, develop to their conclusions entirely within Faeryland. The Faery knights perform no extranational political functions; they seem to be restricted in the operation of their particular virtues to their native land. They are a heterogeneous group of knights including not only the major Faery heroes—Guyon and Calidore—but also all those who serve Gloriana as members of her Order of Maidenhead.[31] As a group they are much more difficult to categorize than the Britons, since their natures reflect the variety of their native land. As individuals, however, they are less complex than the Britons, more like types than fully developed characters. Yet to say this is to over-generalize, because each of the major figures, whether Faery or Briton, has a unique temperament and a complex personality.

Quests begin either in Britain or in Cleopolis, and each is defined by its origin and by its hero. The quests of the Faery knights emerge directly from Cleopolis and concern internal affairs of Faeryland. Guyon and Calidore are sent by Gloriana to resolve social disorders: Guyon must capture Acrasia, who is an accessory to murder and is probably interfering with the work of Gloriana's knights; Calidore must capture the Blatant Beast, whose thousand contentious tongues are wreaking havoc in Faeryland. Guyon and Calidore are, in effect, glorified civil servants laboring to secure domestic tranquillity in a land rife with iniquity. With essential assistance from his guide, the Palmer, Guyon reaches the Bower of Bliss, binds Acrasia, and sends her toward Cleopolis; then, perhaps overstepping his assigned duties, in a "tempest of . . . wrathfulnesse" and "with rigour pittilesse," Guyon ravages the landscape in one of the most problematical actions in *The Faerie Queene* (2.12.83). Calidore, after abandoning his quest to woo Pastorella, finally chains the Blatant Beast and leads his catch through Faeryland. Unfortunately, some time later the beast "broke his yron chaine, / And got into the world at liberty againe" (6.12.38), where "now he raungeth," "Barking and biting" and bothering "Poets" (6.12.40).

The quests of Redcrosse and Artegall also originate in Cleopolis, but they are suited to the British origins of their heroes. Turning from the social and ethical quests of Guyon and Calidore to the religious and political quests of Redcrosse and Artegall is something like turning from what Tasso would call heroic romance to heroic epic, though Spenser consciously avoids categorizing his innovative recombinations of epic, romance, and allegory. Whatever one calls them, the quests that Gloriana assigns to the Britons are proper matter for the "Poet historicall." Both Redcrosse and Artegall must move outside Faeryland to complete their quests, and in each case these passages take them to places that are spatially and temporally distinct representations of historical reality. Redcrosse completes his service to Gloriana in Eden lands by killing the dragon and freeing Una's parents: he defends an ally of the queen of Faeryland, founds the Church of England, and establishes for a moment the new earth of Christ's redemption, a heavy dose of questing compared to Guyon's destruction of the Bower. Artegall goes to Ireland not as a civil servant but as a bringer of political justice and a military emissary from the queen of Faeryland. Spenser spells out the political circumstances involved in Artegall's quest. A suppliant comes to Gloriana seeking aid for Irena,

"Whom a strong tyrant did vniustly thrall, / And from the heritage, which she did clame, / Did with strong hand withhold: *Grantorto* was his name" (5.1.3). The Faery Queen, "Whose glorie is . . . of weake Princes to be Patronesse," chooses Artegall "to right her to restore; / For that to her he seem'd best skild in righteous lore" (5.1.4). Artegall frees Irena from Grantorto—a composite figure representing Spain, Catholicism, Irish rebellion, and general lawlessness—and in so doing enacts an allegory of Elizabeth's policy in Ireland. In a manner analogous to Lord Gray, he attempts "to reforme that ragged common-weale" (5.12.26) by setting loose his "yron man" Talus to "inflict most grieuous punishment" upon all who "did rebell gainst lawfull gouernment" (5.12.26). Like Lord Gray, Artegall is recalled to court "ere he could reforme it thoroughly" (5.12.27).

The quests that proceed from Cleopolis reflect the various roles Gloriana plays in *The Faerie Queene* and the multiple meanings merged in the idea of Cleopolis. The Faeries serve the sovereign of Faeryland, an imaginary country full of enough disorder to keep any ruler busy; their quests, as well as all the action that takes place in Faeryland, are governed by a moral ideal embodied in Gloriana, the Faery Queen of the world of imagination. Since Faeryland exists within a larger world, its queen has responsibilities outside the borders of her realm; these responsibilities she puts in the hands of Britons, not natives of Faeryland. Yet these apparent aliens are in fact Gloriana's countrymen—in the case of Artegall a kinsman—in her role as Elizabeth. Redcrosse serves the head of the Church of England and Artegall the mighty Tudor sovereign, a political ruler in the world of history, not the Faery being capable of appearing to Arthur in a vision. They owe allegiance to a ruler representing an ideal of earthly civil, religious, and political perfection who is a vision of Elizabeth's potential.

Despite the ideal image of Gloriana and her city emphasized throughout the poem, prophecies of perfection seem a long way from being actualized, even when the quests have been accomplished. Like Elizabeth, Gloriana remains the ruler of a troubled land within an equally troubled world and must therefore exert her energy toward immediate political and social concerns, postponing indefinitely the apocalyptic moment. The world in which she rules seems actively to circumvent imaginative perfection. Redcrosse fulfills his duty to Gloriana by killing the dragon, and the king of Eden thinks he deserves a rest:

> For neuer liuing man, I weene, so sore
> In sea of deadly daungers was distrest;
> But since now safe ye seised haue the shore,

And well arriued are, (high God be blest)
Let vs deuize of ease and euerlasting rest.

(1.12.17)

But rather than putting down his arms, as he promises the hermit Contemplation he will do (1.10.64), and rather than marrying Una, thus enacting the mystical marriage of Christ and his Church, Redcrosse must leave Eden lands:

Ah dearest Lord, said then that doughty knight,
Of ease or rest I may not yet deuize;
For by the faith, which I to armes haue plight,
I bounden am streight after this emprize,
As that your daughter can ye well aduize,
Backe to returne to that great Faerie Queene,
And her to serue six yeares in warlike wize,
Gainst that proud Paynim king, that workes her teene:
Therefore I ought craue pardon, till I there haue beene.

Vnhappie falles that hard necessitie,
(Quoth [the king]) the troubler of my happie peace,
And vowed foe of my felicitie;
Ne I against the same can iustly preace.

(1.12.18–19)

Redcrosse leaves Una "to mourne" (1.12.41). Similarly, Artegall fulfills his obligation to Gloriana by freeing Irena from Grantorto, but as knight of justice he desires to reform Irena's "ragged common-weale" (5.12.26). He too, however, must first serve Gloriana's immediate political ends:

But ere he could reforme it thoroughly,
He through occasion called was away,
To Faerie Court, that of necessity
His course of Iustice he was forst to stay,
And *Talus* to reuoke from the right way,
In which he was that Realme for to redresse.
But enuies cloud still dimmeth vertues ray.
So hauing freed *Irena* from distresse,
He tooke his leaue of her, there left in heauinesse.

(5.12.27)

Back in Faeryland he must confront the attacks of Envy, Detraction, and the Blatant Beast, the social enemies of the political hero. And presuming that Artegall, like Redcrosse, is to be enlisted for service in Gloriana's military conflict against the Paynim king, he also must postpone the achievement of his final quest—marriage to Britomart and defense of sixth-century Britain against "The powre of forrein Paynims, which inuade [that] land" (3.3.27).[32]

Unlike the Faery knights, who serve only Gloriana queen of Faeryland, the Britons also serve Elizabeth as her countrymen in foreign affairs and in the process of empire-building. In addition, they owe allegiance to personal destinies—historical, mythical, and romantic—whose ends lie beyond Faeryland and apart from Gloriana's immediate concerns. These personal desires and destinies conflict with while they define the political necessities that govern the actions of a monarch engaged in the business of ruling. The two-fold quests of Redcrosse and Artegall—their destined marriages and their duties to Gloriana—help to define Spenser's epic anatomy of history by creating a pattern of temporal mediations among sixteenth-century English, ancient British, and biblical history. The quests of Arthur and Britomart, which emerge directly from sixth-century Britain, complete this pattern by creating direct links between sixth-century and sixteenth-century history.

3. The Quests from Britain

Spenser sets two crucial episodes of *The Faerie Queene* in Britain. After Arthur frees Redcrosse from Orgoglio's dungeon, he describes to Una and Redcrosse his fostering in North Wales under the tutelage of Merlin and Timon and his vision of the Faery Queen, which lures him toward adventure in Faeryland (1.9.2–16). The narrator supplies a lengthy and detailed account of the inception of Britomart's quest in South Wales, where she falls in love with an image of Artegall in Merlin's magic mirror and hears her historical destiny in Merlin's prophecy (3.2–3). Her love and destiny impel her into Faeryland. Spenser's portrayal of Britomart's experiences in war-ravaged late fifth- or early sixth-century South Wales is unique in *The Faerie Queene*: it is the only sustained representational depiction of socio-political reality in a particular historical place and time. As such, the setting in Britomart's Britain is Spenser's rendering of the traditional heroic epic setting. It is important in several ways to the meaning of *The Faerie Queene*. First, the place Britain defines the idea of Britain better than anything else in the poem. Second, just as the multiform idea of Cleopolis elucidates the quests of Guyon, Calidore, Redcrosse, and Artegall, so the British origins of Arthur's and Britomart's quests help to define their meanings. Third, Spenser's portrayal of life in Britain helps to explain why the psychological constitution of the Britons as a race differs from that of the Faeries. In a word, the Britons are more passionate than the Faeries; they incline naturally toward passion in all its manifestations. Their British blood supplies them with the ardor, determination, and heroic energy necessary to epic heroes. Fourth, Britomart's movement out of Britain and her first encounter in Faeryland—her unhorsing of Guyon—provide a definitive statement of the difference between Britain and Faeryland. And fifth, Britain provides a suggestive perspective from which to view the poet manipulating epic and romance tendencies in his fiction.

Spenser's depiction of the events that occur in Britain represents his most sustained unallegorical invention in *The Faerie Queene*. In the language of the Letter to Ralegh, the action in Britain is historical fiction stripped of the allegorical ornaments that obscure the facts of history. Spenser employs what Renaissance critics call icastic imitation: he provides a likeness or resemblance of life. His fiction is verisimilar because it imitates the probable; even the marvelous things in Britomart's story—the magic mirror Merlin builds and the prophecy he delivers—are what the Italian critics call the marvelous-probable. Britain is a representational rather than an illustrative fiction; it seeks "to reproduce actuality" rather than "to present selected aspects of the actual."[33] The story of Britomart in Britain is a mimetic narrative that becomes an empirical narrative of history when Merlin sets it within his prophetic chronicle.[34] Since Spenser makes Britain the home of his epic heroes and the place whence his two controlling nationalistic quests emerge, he keeps it as closely tied to history and ordinary reality and as free of allegory as his plan allows.

Britomart is a lovesick young princess whose father is away at war. Having failed to cure her with home remedies and white magic, Britomart's nurse, Glauce, takes her to Merlin as a last resort. Although Merlin admits rather jovially that he has no cure for lovesickness, he tells Britomart that it is her destiny to seek Artegall in Faeryland and bring him back to rule Britain. He sends her on her way with the blessing of divine providence. The Britomart of this story is untouched by allegory; we see her moving slowly toward her adventure, but she is not yet the patroness of chastity.

One suggestive difference between the narratives of Britain and Faeryland concerns Spenser's treatment of allegory as a species of fiction that disguises facts. Allegorical disguise, sensible deception by magic, and even physical transformation are the norm in Faeryland, but there is no disguise in the ordinary sense of wearing garments as camouflage to conceal one's identity. Only Artegall wears this kind of disguise in Faeryland when he appears on the tournament grounds in Book 4 as the Salvage Knight and fights against the Knights of Maidenhead (see 4.4.39–44). Significantly, Artegall and Britomart first encounter each other under these circumstances; she ignominiously defeats the Salvage Knight in the name of Maidenhead and takes the tournament prize, leaving Artegall to plot revenge (see 4.4.44; 4.5.9,28–6.23). During the two cantos of British narrative, Britomart and Glauce twice disguise themselves for reasons of practical necessity. When they leave the safety of Britomart's father's castle to seek Merlin's aid, they disguise themselves "in straunge / And base attyre, that none might them bewray" (3.3.7). Since they travel through a war-torn countryside, they wish to appear as peasants rather than as a princess and her nurse. Similarly, they plan "to maske in strange disguise" (3.3.51) as a means of leaving Britain undetected. "At last the Nourse in her foolhardy wit / Conceiu'd a bold deuise": she reasons that since "now all Britanie doth burne in armes bright . . . Let vs in feigned armes our selues disguize" (3.3.52–3). They steal the necessary armor and weapons from King Ryence's war booty,

> Tho to their ready Steeds they clombe full light,
> And through back wayes, that none might them espy,
> Couered with secret cloud of silent night,
> Themselues they forth conuayed, and passed forward right.
>
> Ne rested they, till that to Faery lond
> They came, as *Merlin* them directed late.
>
> (3.3.61–2)

They seek Merlin in "base attyre," but they disguise themselves in armor to seek Artegall in Faeryland. Britomart and Glauce remain disguised, except for the illuminated moments when Britomart doffs her armor to reveal her angelic beauty, but they are the exception rather than the rule in Faeryland. In a way, Britomart's armor is no longer a disguise after she leaves Britain since she becomes a "mayd Martiall" (3.3.53) when she enters Faeryland.

The "glassie globe" (3.2.21) in which Britomart sees an idealized image of Artegall has symbolic importance for the whole poem; but it exists in Britain as a marvelous yet believable magical object that "The great Magitian *Merlin* has deuiz'd, / By his deepe science, and hell-dreaded might" (3.2.18).[35] Merlin is indeed a magician, but as Rosemond Tuve points out, he is "no mere roused spirit"; he is "a known Merlin" who is "a part of England's history."[36] The marvelous "looking glasse" (3.2.18) turns out to be a window through which Britomart looks into her imagination in Faeryland, but the image of Artegall she sees is ideal not because the real Artegall is ideal but because the mirror reflects Britomart's desire (see 3.2.22–5).

Besides being essentially unallegorical, the British narrative is realistic in the way that Chaucer and Shakespeare are realistic, an imitation of life as it is or was rather than as it could be or ought to be. Spenser emphasizes in his portrayal of Britomart's experiences in Britain a mimetic kind of psychological and physiological realism different from the allegorical kind characteristic of Faeryland. Almost everyone in Faeryland is wounded by love (Guyon is the glaring exception), but the attendant pain and frustrated desire usually take allegorical form. No lover in Faeryland suffers in the same way as Britomart does in Britain. She experiences a classical case of lovesickness, protracted and nearly severe enough to kill her. Frightening dreams make sleep impossible; she grows pale, thin, and listless and develops a painful stomach disorder (see 3.2.27–52). Glauce attempts homely herbal cures and even white magic, but to no avail:

> Ne nought it mote the noble Mayd auayle,
> Ne slake the furie of her cruell flame,
> But that she still did waste, and still did wayle,
> That through long languour, and hart-burning brame
> She shortly like a pyned ghost became,
>
> (3.2.52)

What Amoret represents in the House of Busirane—a victim of erotic love as pain—Britomart experiences in Britain (see 3.12.19–21,30–8).

The British setting, like nothing else in *The Faerie Queene*, is homely and domestic, characterized by Britomart's intimate relationship with Glauce and her nurse's tender ministrations of aid and comfort. After a particularly troubling dream, Britomart wakes with a start and Glauce responds:

> Feeling her leape out of her loathed nest,
> Betwixt her feeble armes her quickly keight,
> And downe againe in her warm bed her dight;

Ah my deare daughter, ah my dearest dread,
What vncouth fit (said she) what euill plight
Hath thee opprest, and with sad drearyhead
Chaunged thy liuely cheare, and liuing made thee dead?

(3.2.30)

Glauce comforts her with kind words and then with a compassionate embrace:

So hauing said, her twixt her armes twaine
She straightly straynd, and colled tenderly,
And euery trembling ioynt, and euery vaine
She softly felt, and rubbed busily,
To doe the frosen cold away to fly;
And her faire deawy eies with kisses deare
She oft did bath, and oft againe did dry;
And euer her importund, not to feare
To let the secret of her hart to her appeare.

(3.2.34)

Britomart confesses her love for the image she had seen in the glass. In another incident, Britomart and Glauce go to church seeking aid through prayer, but neither can keep her mind on her devotions (3.2.48). When they finally come before Merlin, Glauce attempts to hide Britomart's lovesickness from the wizard. The results are both humorous and psychologically sound. Glauce begins:

Now haue three Moones with borrow'd brothers light,
Thrice shined faire, and thrice seem'd dim and wan,
Sith a sore euill, which this virgin bright
Tormenteth, and doth plonge in dolefull plight,
First rooting tooke; but what thing it mote bee,
Or whence it sprong, I cannot read aright:
But this I read, that but if remedee
Thou her afford, full shortly I her dead shall see.

Therewith th'Enchaunter softly gan to smyle
At her smooth speeches, weeting inly well,
That she to him dissembled womanish guyle,
And to her said, Beldame, by that ye tell,
More need of leach-craft hath your Damozell,

Then of my skill: who helpe may haue elsewhere,
In vaine seekes wonders out of Magicke spell.
Th'old woman wox half blanck, those words to heare;
And yet was loth to let her purpose plaine appeare.

And to him said, If any leaches skill,
Or other learned meanes could haue redrest
This my deare daughters deepe engraffed ill,
Certes I should be loth thee to molest:
But this sad euill, which doth her infest,
Doth course of naturall cause farre exceed,
And housed is within her hollow brest,
That either seemes some cursed witches deed,
Or euill spright, that in her doth such torment breed.

The wisard could no lenger beare her bord,
But brusting forth in laughter, to her sayd:
Glauce, what needs this colourable word,
To cloke the cause, that hath it self bewrayd?
Ne ye faire *Britomartis*, thus arayd,
More hidden are, then Sunne in cloudy vele;
Whom thy good fortune, hauing fate obayd,
Hath hither brought, for succour to appele:
The which the powres to thee are pleased to reuele.

The doubtfull Mayd, seeing her self descryde,
Was all abasht, and her pure yuory
Into a cleare Carnation suddeine dyde;
As faire *Aurora* rising hastily,
Doth by her blushing tell, that she did lye
All night in old *Tithonus* frosen bed,
Whereof she seems ashamed inwardly.

(3.3.16–20)

Merlin in effect strips away disguises, both of speech and of dress, before revealing his prophecy. He discloses the history of the fiction: fiction stands naked as history. Like all the Britons, Britomart lives in history and must finally live for historical destiny. Spenser sets Britain firmly and specifically in a world of political history and geography. Britomart's father, Ryence, rules "*Deheubarth* that now South-wales is hight" (3.2.18). Britomart's Britain, where Ryence and Uther fight a continuing war against the Saxons, is

Spenser's heroic epic setting, a world of war, political history, and naturalistic description where, after making Britomart blush and hearing another entreaty from Glauce, Merlin unfolds Britomart's historical destiny.

Merlin's prophecy, a select chronicle shaped by Spenser from numerous sources, records British political history from Artegall's death to Elizabeth's reign.[37] Merlin twice breaks into vision. When he describes Malgo, unifier of Wales, he addresses Britomart: "Behold the man, and tell me *Britomart*, / If ay more goodly creature thou didst see" (3.3.32); he sees the man before him, then moves directly back to his narration. At the end of his chronicle, when his narration would become sixteenth-century prophecy, he is overcome by an ecstatic trance:

> Then shall a royall virgin raine, which shall
> Stretch her white rod ouer the *Belgicke* shore,
> And the great Castle smite so sore with all,
> That it shall make him [Philip II] shake, and shortly learne to fall.
>
> But yet the end is not. There *Merlin* stayd,
> As ouercomen of the spirites powre,
> Or other ghastly spectacle dismayd,
> That secretly he saw, yet note discoure:
> Which suddein fit, and halfe extatick stoure
> When the two fearfull women saw, they grew
> Greatly confused in behauioure;
> At last the fury past, to former hew
> He turnd againe, and chearefull looks (as earst) did shew.
>
> (3.3.49–50)

Spenser uses Merlin's chronicle to link sixth-century Britain to sixteenth-century and prophetic Tudor England, and he uses the authority of Merlin's voice to justify a significant fictional alteration of history: Artegall, to some degree at least, replaces Arthur in the British chronicle. Spenser's manipulation of chronicle material obscures events between the reigns of Uther and Constantius, the cousin of Britomart and Artegall's unnamed son, leaving what appears to be a troubling breach in Tudor genealogy.[38] *Briton moniments* ends with Uther's accession to the throne:

> After him *Vther*, which *Pendragon* hight,
> Succeding There abruptly it did end,
> Without full point, or other Cesure right,

As if the rest some wicked hand did rend,
Or th'Authour selfe could not at least attend
To finish it.

(2.10.68)

Merlin begins his prophecy by revealing to Britomart her successful search for Artegall in Faeryland:

From thence, him firmly bound with faithfull band,
To this his natiue soyle thou backe shalt bring,
Strongly to aide his countrey, to withstand
The powre of forrein Paynims, which inuade thy land.

(3.3.27)

Merlin tells Britomart that she and Artegall will fight wars in Britain side by side,

Till thy wombes burden thee from them do call,
And his last fate him from thee take away,
Too rathe cut off by practise criminall
Of secret foes, that him shall make in mischiefe fall.

(3.3.28)

Artegall will leave Britomart "his Image dead," a son who "from the head / Of his coosin *Constantius* without dread / Shall take the crowne, that was his fathers right" (3.3.29). Apparently, Artegall never claims a crown and Uther dies without an heir, which means that Spenser excises from Tudor genealogical history even a pseudo-Arthurian kingship. Or perhaps, alternatively, Artegall inherits a kingship from King Ryence, Britomart's father; consolidates his Welsh power through Uther; and leaves his son to unite Celtic Britain by wresting the Cornish crown from the son of Cador, Artegall's uncle. Spenser leaves the issue unclear, enabling him to free Arthur from ancient British history and thus coordinate his epic quests; Arthur becomes, in Spenser's altered history, not Elizabeth's ancestor but rather her destined mate. He moves out of sixth-century Britain, through Faeryland, and on to Cleopolis, there to marry Gloriana and fulfill the prophecy of Arthur's return; his marriage to Gloriana would in effect merge sixth- and sixteenth-century history, creating the all-time of the Tudor apocalypse. Simultaneously, the marriage of Redcrosse to Una would parallel in prophetic religious history Arthur's marriage to Gloriana, and Britomart and Artegall, through their son, would found the Tudor line in sixth-century Britain.

Some set of circumstances, perhaps including his untimely death, kept Spenser from completing his epic design. But his plan, outlined in the Letter to Ralegh and hinted at in the poem, seems fairly clear. It calls for twelve books—of which he wrote six and part of a seventh—fashioning the "priuate morall vertues" followed by twelve more that would "frame the . . . pollliticke vertues." According to the Letter, the twelfth book of the first part would treat, as flashback, Gloriana's annual feast, during which the quests emerging from Cleopolis would be initiated. Spenser does not outline his plans in detail, but some speculation is possible. During the first book of the second part, all the heroes, including Arthur and Britomart, would descend upon Cleopolis. Arthur would be betrothed to Gloriana; and the heroes, with Arthur as their leader, would set out on the great military expedition against the terrible Paynim king, which would last six years (see 1.12.18) and probably serve as subject for most of the second twelve books.[39] Spenser refers to this part of his poetic labor in two places. Immediately before narrating Redcrosse's fight with the dragon, the poet pauses to invoke his "sacrd Muse," Clio:

O gently come into my feeble brest,
  Come gently, but not with that mighty rage,
  Wherewith the martiall troupes thou doest infest,
  And harts of great Heroes doest enrage,
  That nought their kindled courage may aswage,
  Soone as thy dreadfull trompe begins to sownd;
  The God of warre with his fiers equipage
  Thou doest awake, sleepe neuer he so sownd,
And scared nations doest with horrour sterne astownd.

Faire Goddesse lay that furious fit aside,
  Till I of warres and bloudy *Mars* do sing,
  And Briton fields with Sarazin bloud bedyde,
  Twixt that great faery Queene and Paynim king,
  That with their horrour heauen and earth did ring,
  A worke of labour long, and endlesse prayse:
  But now a while let downe that haughtie string,
  And to my tunes thy second tenor rayse,
That I this man of God his godly armes may blaze.

(1.11.6–7)

In his dedicatory sonnet to Essex, Spenser refers to a time when his muse "With bolder wing shall dare alofte to sty / To the last praises of this Faery Queene." In this later narrative, Spenser explains, he will praise the military and political virtues embodied in the Earl of Essex.[40]

After the war, Gloriana's knights would return in victorious triumph to Cleopolis; the marriage of Arthur and Gloriana in Cleopolis would coincide with that of Redcrosse and Una in Eden lands. As for Britomart and Artegall, they would probably have returned to Britain, either married or officially betrothed, at the beginning of the second twelve books; their war against sixth-century paynims would thus parallel Arthur's war against sixteenth-century paynims. Spenser's monumental, unrealized epic could conceivably have had a dual ending: in Cleopolis and Eden lands, the end would be high comic prophecy; in Britain, the end would be heroic and prophetic yet tragic, with Artegall "Too rathe cut off by practise criminall" (3.3.28). Spenser's plan was to combine the three Virgilian epic quests he found implicit in the *Aeneid.* The quest of Britomart and Artegall corresponds to Aeneas's primary nationalistic quest: the wars which Aeneas fights in Latium parallel those which Britomart and Artegall were to fight in Britain; Aeneas establishes the Augustan line as Britomart and Artegall were to establish the Tudor. The realization of Arthur's quest would have taken Anchises' prophecy of Augustan Rome one step further, beyond the poet's time toward the prophetic future of an apocalyptic third Troy. The quest of Redcrosse, even as it stands, corresponds to the Christian allegorical reading of the *Aeneid* as the spiritual pilgrimage of the Christian hero.[41]

Before allowing Britomart to move the discussion away from the Britain of the poem, I want to note a curious circumstance concerning the British narratives, especially the story of Britomart but also those of Arthur, Artegall, Redcrosse, and Tristram. Spenser composes the British narratives almost entirely of material borrowed from other authors, including Virgil, Chaucer, Ariosto, Malory, and the British historians. The material he chooses out of these authors, excluding the historians, seems curious stuff for the epic poet to use in filling out his heroic setting. Spenser builds his British narratives out of source materials that contrast sharply with the heroic epic setting in which Artegall is destined to be murdered.[42]

Most of the interchange between Glauce and Britomart (3.2.30–51) Spenser translates and adapts from the romantic and tragic pseudo-Virgilian epyllion *Ciris*, the tale of Scylla, the king of Crete's daughter, whose passion for Minos, the besieger of her father's city, drives her to betray her father. Scylla and her father are victims of the bloodbath that follows her betrayal. Spenser borrows from the pivotal scene between Scylla and her nurse, Carme.[43] Spenser borrows the magic mirror belonging to Britomart's father from Chaucer's *Squire's Tale*, a parody of the popular metrical romances.[44] Similarly, Spenser adapts Arthur's story of his vision of the Faery Queen from Chaucer the pilgrim's *Tale of Sir Thopas*, Chaucer the poet's most blatant parody of romance conventions.[45] Spenser borrows from Malory certain details concerning Arthur's upbringing in Britain (1.9.3–5) and Tristram's in Lyonesse (6.2.28–30).[46] The stories of the thefts of Redcrosse and Artegall by fairies (1.10.65; 3.3.26) are conventional romance fare. Finally, Spenser borrows from Ariosto the idea of having his heroine receive a prophecy of her descendants from Merlin, but there are few details common to the two accounts.[47]

Spenser adapts his romance sources to serve his epic design. The homely realism of Virgil's account of Scylla and Carme perfectly fits Spenser's British setting, but Spenser turns a lust-crazed Scylla into his chaste heroine.[48] He turns a magic mirror that is little more than a conventional prop in *The Squire's Tale* into a "glassie globe" that reflects Britomart's desire and provides her first unconscious glimpse of her historical destiny. Spenser transforms what Chaucer's Host calls the "'drasty rymyng'" of *Sir Thopas* into an arresting vision that moves Arthur toward his unknown destiny.[49] Spenser's Merlin is a lively, loving, jovial yet powerful being who recites a prophecy; Ariosto's Merlin is a disembodied voice that speaks to Bradamante out of a tomb; the voice instructs an enchantress to command spirits, which take the forms of Bradamante's and Ruggiero's descendants.

Spenser creates his epic setting in Britain by manipulating romance source materials, and he uses Britain in conjunction with Faeryland to accomplish a thorough and innovative merging of epic and romance. Britomart's move from Britain into Faeryland illustrates Spenser's purpose. As long as she stays in Britain, she remains little more than a lovesick young woman. Like the British setting, composed primarily of conventional romance matter that the poet invests with epic potential, Britomart possesses *in potentia* the attributes of an epic heroine. But during her experiences in Britain, she is a weakened and troubled damsel in distress whose desires are erotic, not heroic. She seems to listen attentively to Merlin's prophecy of her future husband's untimely death, the woeful and bloody defeat of the Britons by the Saxons, and the eventual reestablishment of the British nation. Yet, after witnessing Merlin's frightening ecstatic fit, she seems to forget everything but the knowledge that her beloved is in Faeryland. Without acknowledging the hard trials of historical destiny that Merlin unfolds, Britomart and Glauce leave Merlin's cave "both conceiuing hope of comfort glad, / With lighter hearts vnto their home retird" (3.3.51), where they ready themselves for their journey to Faeryland.

Britomart and Glauce steal disguises from Ryence's war booty, and Glauce dresses Britomart in the armor of the Saxon queen Angela. "As a Briton maid dressed in the armor of a Saxon maid (especially a Saxon maid who *names* her people), Britomart becomes herself an image or type of the resolution that, as Merlin prophesies, must be the end of centuries of conflict. In the armor she appears a fusion of the two dominant peoples whose conflict occupies Merlin's prophecy."[50] Although Britomart's physical attributes reflect her martial potential, Glauce knows she is yet unskilled in arms:

> Ne certes daughter that same warlike wize
> I weene, would you misseeme; for ye bene tall,
> And large of limbe, t'atchieue an hard emprize,
> Ne ought ye want, but skill, which practize small
> Will bring, and shortly make you a mayd Martiall.
>
> (3.3.53)

The uninitiated maiden warrior and her nurse sneak out of Britain in disguise and under cover of darkness, and the one thing on Britomart's mind is fulfillment of her romantic desire. These circumstances bear little resemblance to those described in Britomart's dissembling speech to Redcrosse:

> Faire Sir, I let you weete, that from the howre
> I taken was from nourses tender pap,
> I haue beene trained vp in warlike stowre,
> To tossen speare and shield, and to affrap
> The warlike ryder to his most mishap;
> Sithence I loathed haue my life to lead,
> As Ladies wont, in pleasures wanton lap,
> To finger the fine needle and nyce thread;
> Me leuer were with point of foemans speare be dead.
>
> All my delight on deeds of armes is set,
> To hunt out perils and aduentures hard,
> By sea, by land, where so they may be met,
> Onely for honour and for high regard,
> Without respect of richesse or reward.
> For such intent into these parts I came,
> Withouten compasse, or withouten card,

> Far fro my natiue soyle, that is by name
> The greater *Britaine*, here to seeke for prayse and fame.
>
> (3.2.6–7)

She tells Redcrosse that she seeks "Tydings of one, that hath vnto me donne / Late foule dishonour and reprochful spight, / The which I seeke to wreake, and *Arthegall* he hight" (3.2.8). This is all psychologically satisfying, but it is not entirely true.

Britomart leaves Britain as a young maiden in love; she bursts upon the scene in Faeryland, without even the "practize small" that Glauce admits she needs, as a royal and warlike maid who is the allegorical patroness of chastity. She is still young and in love, and her temperament never changes, but Faeryland gives her something more: it invests her with an allegorical strength while it nurtures her spirit. In her first encounter in Faeryland, she humiliatingly and effortlessly unhorses the Knight of Temperance and takes part, along with Arthur and Guyon, in an allegorical rite of reconciliation that creates a background for the action of Books 3 and 4 (see 3.1.6–13). In her next encounter, she rescues Redcrosse from no less than six knights, who seek to force him to serve Malecasta, "*Lady of delight*" (3.1.21–24,31). They ignore her spoken entreaties, "Till that she rushing through the thickest preasse, / Perforce disparted their compacted gyre" (3.1.23). Inside Castle Joyous, Malecasta, thinking Britomart a handsome man, steals to her bedroom and climbs into her bed. Changing position in her sleep, Britomart awakens when she feels another body, leaps from her bed, and grabs her sword. Malecasta screams, and everyone in the castle comes running to the door of Britomart's room. What they witness is Britomart undisguised, yet full of heroic might:

> On th'other side, they saw the warlike Mayd
> All in her snow-white smocke with locks vnbownd,
> Threatning the point of her auenging blade,
> That with so troublous terrour they were all dismayde.
>
> (3.1.63)

One of Malecasta's knights wounds Britomart,

> Wherewith enrag'd she fiercely at them flew,
> And with her flaming sword about her layd,
> That none of them foule mischiefe could eschew,
> But with her dreadfull strokes were all dismayd:

> Here, there, and euery where about her swayd
> Her wrathfull steele, that none mote it abide.
>
> (3.1.66)

Britomart's heroic potential derives from her British blood, but it is nurtured and put to work in Faeryland, the allegorical world of romance adventure. Like Arthur, she is driven into and through Faeryland not by historical destiny but by love; Arthur never knows his destiny, and Britomart is wont to forget hers (see 3.4.11–2). Not until her vision at the Temple of Isis does she fully accept her prophetic and tragic fate (see 5.7.12–24), whereupon she rescues Artegall from Radigund and leaves the narrative of Faeryland. She will marry Artegall and fight wars of unification in her native land; Arthur will marry Gloriana and fight wars in defense of Faeryland. Spenser coordinates epic and romance quests by making marriage and nation-building mutually dependent, and he creates a multiform setting consistent with his purpose.

Notes
Chapter IV

1. Sir Thomas Malory, *The Tale of King Arthur*, in *Malory: Works*, 2nd ed., ed. Eugene Vinaver, (1954; rpt. New York: Oxford Univ. Press, 1977), I.i., 5.

2. *The Faerie Queene*, ed. Hamilton, 737.

3. Greenlaw, "Fairy Mythology," 105–22. In this article and others, and in *Studies in Spenser's Historical Allegory*, Greenlaw laid the foundation for modern study of the relation of history to *The Faerie Queene*. In *Historical Allegory* he employs a distinction between historical allusion and historical allegory that has been especially influential.

4. Greenlaw, "Fairy Myth," 107.

5. Greenlaw, "Fairy Myth," 120.

6. Greenlaw, "Fairy Myth," 121. Confusion persists to this day concerning the terminology Spenser adopts to name the places that compose the setting of his poem. For example, while discussing the emerging sense of nationhood among the Elizabethans, Richard Helgerson uses Spenser, among others, to illustrate the various names used by the Elizabethans to describe their nation: "Spenser's England was alternatively 'Britayne land' and 'Faery lond'" (*Forms of Nationhood*, 8). Helgerson either ignores or is

unaware of the explicit distinctions Spenser draws between Britain and Faeryland, both as places and as concepts.

7. See *OED* under Britain and Britany; they are equivalent. Bretange=the lesser Britain; Wales=the greater Britain. Spenser sometimes uses Britany for rhyme.

8. Spenser also outlines the border between Faeryland and Picteland: "And Twede the limit betwixt Logris land / And Albany" (4.11.36). Spenser mentions no rivers north of the Tweed; he apparently conceives of a united England composed of the British Isles minus Scotland. He is probably being practical. The only place in *The Faerie Queene* that may be in Scotland is the "Castle of *Belgard*" (6.12.3), where Calidore takes Pastorella after rescuing her from the Brigants. There Pastorella discovers her lost parents, Bellamoure and Claribell. Claribell's father had been the "Lord of *Many Ilands*" (6.12.4) before his death. He had wanted Claribell to marry "the Prince of *Picteland* bordering nere" (6.12.4), but she conceives Pastorella by Bellamoure instead. Pastorella is abandoned and reared by Meliboe. Claribell and Bellamoure remain in Claribell's father's castle, apparently in western Scotland, and this is where Calidore brings Pastorella.

9. Hamilton, ed., *The Faerie Queene*, annotation to 4.11.39.

10. Hough, 129.

11. Berger, *The Allegorical Temper*, 171.

12. Berger, *Temper*, 167–9.

13. Roche, *Flame*, 45–6.

14. Roche, 32–5.

15. Roche, 45.

16. See Roche, 32.

17. Roche, 49.

18. Michael O'Connell, *Mirror and Veil*, 81, is rather too categorical in distinguishing the idea of Britain from Faeryland: "The significance of the contrast of the *Briton moniments* to the Faery chronicle is not just the contrast of the uncertainty of the actual to the orderliness of the ideal but also that the ideal is embodied in a fictional world [Faeryland]. Fiction amends the actual and thereby makes it ideal." Other critics who allow for the existence of the idea of Britain while emphasizing the ideality of Faeryland make similar claims.

19. Berger, *Temper*, 104–5. Compare Berger, "The Prospect of Imagination: Spenser and the Limits of Poetry," *Studies in English Literature* 1 (1961): 97; and MacCaffrey, *Spenser's Allegory*, 60–70.

20. Greenlaw, "Fairy Myth," 118; Rathborne, *Meaning*, 141–54.

21. Berger, *Temper*, 110–11. Compare Hume, *Protestant Poet*, 59–71, 146–9.

22. Berger, "The Spenserian Dynamics," *Studies in English Literature* 8 (1968): 17.

23. Berger, *Temper*, 109.

24. This is Berger's main thesis concerning Guyon in *The Allegorical Temper*. He provides a similar account of Calidore in "The Prospect of Imagination."

25. Berger, "Prospect," 101–2.

26. Horton, *Unity*, 126–30.

27. Fletcher, *Prophetic Moment*, 88. Donald Cheney, *Spenser's Image of Nature: Wild Man and Shepherd in* The Faerie Queene (New Haven: Yale Univ. Press, 1966), makes a similar point but carries it too far. He says the Faeries are "untouched by the burden of Time in the Christian sense of the word" (8) and therefore unfallen and unredeemed; the Britons are "fortunately fallen out of Eden and into a Christian dispensation" (43). Thus, Jove "balances accounts" in Faeryland (66). (Does Jove send the angel to aid Guyon?)

28. MacCaffrey, 76.

29. To my knowledge, Berger never makes an explicit distinction between the place Britain and the place Faeryland. What he says is rather ambiguous: "Since, in the poem's total vision, no ontological distinction can be made between historical Britain and mythical Faery—since both have equal and complementary dramatic functions—one cannot legitimately distinguish 'levels of meaning' which are actually separable" (*Temper*, 167). Depending upon what he means by "ontological" and "'levels of meaning,'" I either agree or disagree. MacCaffrey recognizes that Britomart is in a different place from Faeryland during her time in Britain, but she claims that "the quality of the events there rehearsed do [sic] not differ noticeably from those in 'Fairy Land'" (71 n. 12). I disagree. To this day, the only critic I know of who has made substantial use of Britain as a distinct place in *The Faerie Queene* is Rathborne (in 1937).

30. Cheney, 121, notes that "visitors to Fairyland . . . are bound to the responsibilities of their historical roles." O'Connell, 72, remarks on the Britons' "responsibility to history" and goes on to compare them to Aeneas and other epic heroes. See also Fletcher, *Prophetic Moment*, 147.

31. On membership in the Order of Maidenhead, an allusion to the Order of the Garter, see 1.7.46; 2.2.42, 9.6; 3.8.46–7; 4.4.17–48; 5.4.29,34. See also Michael Leslie, *Spenser's "Fierce Warres and Faithfull Loves": Martial and Chivalric Symbolism in* The Faerie Queene (Totowa, NJ: Barnes and Noble, 1983), 132–58.

32. Paynims are literally pagans, non-Christians, but Spenser uses the term to name generally the enemies of his heroes. Sixth-century paynims

include Saxons and perhaps Scandinavian invaders; sixteenth-century paynims include Roman Catholics (see 1.11.7; 3.3.52).

33. Scholes and Kellogg, *Nature of Narrative*, 88. I draw from the following statements: "Illustration differs from representation in narrative art in that it does not seek to reproduce actuality but to present selected aspects of the actual, essences referable for their meaning not to historical, psychological, or sociological truth but to ethical and metaphysical truth" (88). "The illustrative is symbolic; the representational is mimetic" (84). Scholes and Kellogg note that the "epic apparatus of *The Faerie Queene* . . . is the main representational vehicle for the illustrative 'other' meaning of Spenser's highly intellectualized allegory" (111). My analysis of Britain and the epic quests is in essential agreement with these statements.

34. See Scholes and Kellogg, 105–6, 147. Epic narrative is empirical insofar as it is related to history and mimetic insofar as it is fictional. Scholes and Kellogg provide another kind of distinction during their discussion of traditional epic narrative. "The distinction between fact and fiction, once it is clearly established, forces story-telling to choose the rubric under which it will function: truth or beauty. The result is a separation of narrative streams into factual and fictional, producing forms we have learned to call history and romance" (58). Since "epic poems are made in cultures which do not distinguish between myth and history," epic narrative falls under the rubric of truth, fact, or history (57–8).

Considering Spenser's studies as an antiquary-historian, in which he was beginning to note distinctions as well as relationships between myth and history, his decision to combine romance and epic seems natural and consistent. Spenser's decision bears interesting contrast to Milton's decision to reject British subject matter for his epic.

35. On the "world of glas" (3.2.19) as a symbol for the world of fiction, see Williams, *World of Glass*, xvii, 94–5, et passim; MacCaffrey, 304, 403–4; and Dunseath, *Spenser's Allegory*, 18–20. The globe of glass "signifies fragile marital harmony in Renaissance iconography" (Hamilton, ed., *The Faerie Queene*, annotation to 3.2.18.8). For accounts of Elizabethan belief in the magical powers of spheres of beryl and various mirrors, see *Variorum*, 3:216–7.

36. Tuve, *Allegorical Imagery*, 95.

37. Spenser's major sources are the chronicles of Geoffrey of Monmouth, Raphael Holinshed, John Stow, and John Hardyng. The definitive study of Spenser's use of chronicle material remains Carrie A. Harper's *The Sources of the British Chronicle History in Spenser's* Faerie Queene (Philadelphia, 1910). See *Variorum* 2:32–8, 449–55; 3:228–35. See also Josephine Waters Bennett, *The Evolution of* The Faerie Queene (Chi-

cago: Univ. of Chicago Press, 1942), 61–79, 88–92; Harry Berger, Jr., "The Structure of Merlin's Chronicle in *The Faerie Queene* III (iii)," *Studies in English Literature* 9 (1969): 38–51.

38. See Hamilton, ed., *The Faerie Queene*, annotation to 3.3.27,29; *Variorum* 3:228–9; Rathborne, 223–30.

39. In "The Projected Continuation of *The Faerie Queene*: *Rome Delivered*?" (*Spenser Studies* 8 [1990]: 335–42), A. Kent Hieatt presents convincing evidence that Spenser's long-range plans included Arthur's conquering Rome and being crowned emperor.

40. Text from Hamilton, ed., *The Faerie Queene*, 741. In the sonnet to Essex, Spenser speaks in the same public voice as he does in the Letter to Ralegh.

Magnificke Lord, whose vertues excellent
  Doe merit a most famous Poets witt,
  To be thy liuing praises instrument,
  Yet do not sdeigne, to let thy name be writt
In this base Poeme, for thee far vnfitt.
  Nought is thy worth disparaged thereby,
  But when my Muse, whose fethers nothing flitt
  Doe yet but flagg, and lowly learne to fly
With bolder wing shall dare alofte to sty
  To the last praises of this Faery Queene,
  Then shall it make more famous memory
  Of thine Heroicke parts, such as they beene:
Till then vouchsafe thy noble countenaunce
  To these first labours needed furtheraunce.

41. See E.M.W. Tillyard, *Epic*, 100, 134–35; Murrin, *Allegorical Epic*, 27–50.

42. The exception, which fits Spenser's epic purpose, is the resemblance between some of Merlin's words to Britomart and the words of the Sibyl to Aeneas. See Hughes, *Virgil and Spenser*, 354–7. See commentary on other sources in *Variorum* 3:216 (Chaucer), 225 (Malory), 370 (Ariosto). On Spenser's use of Chaucer's *Tale of Sir Thopas*, see Bennett, *Evolution*, 11–5, 18–23, 29–30.

43. See Hughes, *Virgil and Spenser*, 348–54, for a comparison of Spenser's and Virgil's texts. I paraphrase Hughes's plot summary of the *Ciris*. See also Roche, 53–5.

44. Compare *The Faerie Queene*, 3.2.19–20, with *Squire's Tale*, lines 132–45, in *The Complete Poetry and Prose of Geoffrey Chaucer*, ed. John H.

Fisher (New York: Holt, Rinehart, and Winston, 1977), 190. All references to Chaucer are to this edition.

45. Compare Arthur's description of his youthful character (1.9.9–11) with Chaucer's description of Troilus (*Troylus and Criseyde*, I.183–203).

46. See Malory, ed., Vinaver, *The Tale of King Arthur*, I.i–v, 3–9, concerning Arthur; *The Book of Sir Tristram de Lyones*, I.i–ii, 229–30, concerning Tristram.

47. Compare *The Faerie Queene*, 3.3.21–3, with *Orlando Furioso*, trans. Harington, ed. Hough, 3.17–9.

48. Spenser borrows the scene between Glauce and Britomart from Virgil's scene between Carme and Scylla, but Britomart's name he borrows from Carme's virgin daughter Britomartis, who flees into the sea to escape the love of Minos. See Hughes, 354; Roche, 54.

Spenser may be using his source in another way. Scylla loves her father's enemy; Britomart's father, Ryence, is ally to Uther, who is the enemy of Artegall's dead father, Gorlois. This makes Britomart the lover of the son of her father's ally's enemy; thus, by extension, Britomart, like Scylla, loves her father's enemy. Parents' political squabbles seem to be resolved in Faeryland.

49. Compare *The Faerie Queene*, 1.9.9–15, with *The Tale of Sir Thopas*, lines 742–80.

50. O'Connell, 84; cf. Roche, 62.

Epilogue: Stranded in Faeryland

The places Spenser locates outside Faeryland compose *The Faerie Queene*'s heroic epic setting in political and religious history, providing various perspectives on Tudor history and, in conjunction with Faeryland, allowing Spenser to manipulate genre in original ways. In Eden lands, Redcrosse enacts biblical history and re-establishes the dominion of the primitive church. In war-torn sixth-century Wales, Arthur and Britomart fall in love with the providential projections of their desire, and Spenser integrates romance and epic strategies by bringing erotic desire into alignment with historical destiny. In the ocean around Proteus's den, Spenser stages the mythological river marriage that allegorizes the peaceful coexistence of England, Wales, and Ireland. In the land of the Amazon Radigund, Britomart orchestrates the recovery of patriarchal political power. At the court of Mercilla, Arthur and Artegall assist in the conviction of Mary Stuart while Mercilla acts out merciful justice with a few tears, a delay, and "more then needfull naturall remorse" (5.10.4). In Belgium and Ireland, respectively, Arthur and Artegall perform the queen's work in international affairs, enacting allegorical fantasies of imperial power. And at the seat of awesome sovereign power in Cleopolis, Gloriana directs the national and international activities of her army of loyal and submissive knights. In all these places, Spenser depicts fictional and allegorical accounts of political history, the products of historical destiny, sovereign control, and imperial conquest.

The setting outside Faeryland also provides an appropriate fictional space for heroic epic closure: for the destined imperial war against the "Paynim king" (1.11.7), for the wars of Britomart and Artegall in Britain, and for the apocalyptic marriages of Redcrosse to Una in Eden lands and Arthur to Gloriana in Cleopolis. Such suitably glorious acts of closure never occur because, for whatever reason, Spenser never got that far. Instead, Spenser writes several unresolved conclusions in his portrayals of the major characters' final appearances in the narrative; and he writes an ending for Book 6 that serves as a satisfyingly consistent conclusion to the whole poem. In his final depictions of the main heroes and, often, in the actions following the successful achievement of their quests and leading up to their final appearances, Spenser qualifies the heroes' apparent successes and leaves them—particularly the Britons—stranded in Faeryland, variously sad, perplexed, helpless, and disillusioned. Taken together, the final actions—or, more often, non-actions—of the heroes create a tone of somber pathos and irresolution much closer to the tone of the *Aeneid* than would have been created by the glorious triumphs Spenser advertises as the destined ends of his unwritten heroic epic.

After killing the dragon, receiving the adulation of the crowd, and feasting in celebration with the king and queen of Eden lands, Redcrosse responds to the king's "demaund" to tell his story by reciting a "point to point" account of his "voyage long" (1.12.15), conveniently omitting any reference to his dalliance with Duessa. Within minutes, just as the king is about to announce the banns of marriage between Una and Redcrosse, Archimago bursts into the hall and reads Duessa's letter, which exposes Redcrosse's apparent deception and prompts the king to solicit an explanation from his future son-in-law. Redcrosse admits that he "strayd," but both he and Una blame the "wicked arts" and "wylie skill" of "that false sorceresse," and Redcrosse lamely defends his omission by claiming that "day should [have] faile[d]" him if he had included all the "mishaps" that had befallen him (1.12.31-3). The king, "greatly moued" (1.12.35) by Una's defense of her knight and her exposure of Archimago's identity, takes the magician into custody and initiates the betrothal ceremony. These anticlimactic events force Spenser's readers to question the extent of Redcrosse's reformation; furthermore, depending upon the exact nature of the sexual act committed by Redcrosse when, unarmed, drugged, and "Pourd out in loosnesse on the grassy grownd," he made "goodly court" to Duessa (1.7.7), the sanctity and legality of the betrothal might be called into question. Whatever the case may be, Book 1 ends in sadness, for after some time spent "swimming in [a] sea of blissfull ioy," Redcrosse leaves Una "to mourne" (1.12.40–1), postponing the consummation of his marriage for six years while he serves Gloriana "in warlike wize" (1.12.18). Incidentally, Redcrosse seems to have forgotten his promise to the hermit Contemplation: that after assisting Una he would forgo love and arms, return to the Mount of Contemplation, and "walke . . . in Pilgrims poore estate" (1.10.64).

Redcrosse appears in three more episodes before leaving the narrative of Faeryland. In the beginning of Book 2, he has an almost disastrous encounter with Guyon, tricked by Archimago into thinking that Redcrosse had abused a lady, here played by a disguised Duessa. Archimago—like Redcrosse, recently back in Faeryland from Eden lands (see 2.1.1)—here seeks renewed vengeance after having his suit on Duessa's behalf treated as fraud by Una's father. His newly hatched scheme fails when, at the last moment, Guyon realizes his error and avoids a clash with Redcrosse. When Redcrosse next appears, he is "beset on euery side" by Malecasta's knights until Britomart, "rushing through the thickest preasse, / Perforce dispart[s] their compacted gyre," freeing Redcrosse from their attack (3.1.21,23). Although Redcrosse convincingly explains to Britomart that his fidelity to Una forbids him from serving Malecasta, the allegorical context of Book 3 leaves open the possibility that his own erotic desire, which has given him trouble in the past and which he knows he must suppress for six years, implicates him in his predicament. Finally, just before leaving the narrative, Redcrosse listens to Britomart malign Artegall, who she says has done her "foule dishonour and reprochful spight," "beguil[ing]" her, a "simple mayd, and work[ing] so haynous tort," charges that suggest seduction or, at worst, attempted rape (3.2.8,12). Redcrosse defends Artegall with glowing praise, much to Britomart's delight, but he never hears the story that makes Britomart's charges against Artegall psychologically satisfying to Spenser's readers: the narrator's two cantos of flashback describing Britomart's falling in love and visiting Merlin in Britain. Considering what he does hear, Redcrosse must leave the poem confused and disillusioned, anticipating nothing but the prospect of six years of war.

Britomart also exits the narrative in a state of emotional distress, though for somewhat different reasons than Redcrosse. Lovesick young girl, valiant and powerful warrior, loyal betrothed of Artegall, and Spenser's most fully realized protagonist, Britomart controls the narrative for much of Books 3, 4, and 5; but when she leaves the poem (5.7.45), she is grief-stricken and, for the first time in her long journey, not sure where she wants to go or which way is "forward" (see 3.1.19, 3.61-2, 4.5). Having killed Radigund in perhaps the most vicious fight in *The Faerie Queene*, Britomart "break[s] open with indignant ire" the "yron prison . . . In which her wretched loue [is] captiue layd" (5.7.37). Shocked, appalled, and "abasht with secrete shame" to see Artegall dressed in women's clothes, Britomart appears more perplexed here than anywhere else in the poem, astonished beyond her capacity to comprehend what could have "wrought" the "wondrous change" that "robde" her knight of his "manly hew" and made his "great courage stoup." If this can happen, she says, "Then farewell fleshly force; I see thy pride is nought" (5.7.38,40). Painfully aware of her man's—of men's—essential weakness, Britomart takes charge: she strips Artegall of his "vncomely weedes," dresses him in armor, turns political power over to the men, and makes them "sweare fealty to *Artegall*" (5.7.41,43). Before long, Artegall once again abandons Britomart, once again proceeding on "his first aduenture" to do the queen's work (5.7.43). Britomart, although "Full sad and sorrowfull," knows he is doing what any man in military service must do, so she wishes him "successe" and represses her "griefe" (5.7.44). But after "a certaine space . . . his want her woe did more increase" until, "hoping that the change of aire and place / Would change her paine, and sorrow somewhat ease," Britomart leaves the city and leaves the poem, "her anguish to appease" (5.7.45). She may be looking forward to marriage and a return to Britain with Artegall, but she also knows the rest that Merlin told her: she and Artegall have wars to fight, and she will have a son to bring up on her own after Artegall is murdered (see 3.3.27-9). She does not seem to be left with much hope of appeasing her anguish any time soon.

In his final appearances, Artegall may not be filled with anguish or, for that matter, with any deep emotion, to which his military and judicial training seem to have made him immune. But such is Artegall: crude, vengeful, ruthless, arrogant, rather simple-minded about love, and probably striking in his armor. He is a loyal soldier and judicator, loved by Britomart; he is someone who shows up at Satyrane's tournament dressed in a "quyent disguise" and advertising himself as "*Saluagesse sans finesse*" (4.4.39); he may have allowed his executioner, Talus, to get a little out of hand in Ireland; and he is probably angry and frustrated when he leaves the poem, though he would not dare show it.

After a brief stop in France to deal with Burbon, Artegall sails to Ireland, where he successfully completes his assigned duty to Gloriana by dispatching Grantorto. Intent on pursuing a more thorough solution to Irena's distress, he undertakes "to reforme that ragged common-weale" (5.12.26). To this end, he sends Talus "through all that realme" with orders to "inflict most grieuous punishment" upon all those "that vsd to rob and steale, / Or did rebell gainst lawfull gouernment" (5.12.26). Artegall employs an ancient military and imperial strategy that remains to this day moderately successful: reformation by intimidation, counter-revolution by pacification, conquest by massacre. "But ere he could reforme it thoroughly, / He through occasion called [is] away, / To Faerie Court"; apparently, Gloriana either lost her nerve or disapproved of his "course of Iustice," as Elizabeth did Lord Gray's. Artegall leaves Irena "in heauinesse" (5.12.27), much the same state in which he had left Britomart and in which Redcrosse had left Una. Back in Faeryland, Artegall is accosted by and ignores Envy and Detraction, allegorical aspects of the Blatant Beast, which accompanies them. It may be arrogance or cynicism or stoic self-control that makes Artegall seem "to take no keepe" of his assailants and to forbid Talus from flailing the Blatant Beast (5.12.42,43); he tells Calidore that he ignored the Blatant Beast's attacks because he "knew [himself] from perill free" (6.1.9). But perhaps Artegall's lack of reaction exposes another possibility. Although Spenser's narrator calls the Beast's heinous charges "most vntrew" (5.12.42), the same charges of ruthless cruelty might, as with Lord Gray, be the reasons for Artegall's recall in the first place. From this perspective, the beasts are, in effect, emissaries of the court or, indeed, of Gloriana herself, which would make Artegall's response to them an act of loyalty and would suggest a subversive relationship between the court and the Blatant Beast just before readers turn the page to Book 6. When they turn the page, they meet Artegall for the last time, telling Calidore about his sighting of the Blatant Beast. Here, in contrast to the end of Book 5, the narrator comments upon Artegall's emotional state: when Calidore meets him, Artegall is "returning yet halfe sad / from his late conquest" (6.1.4).

Arthur appears in the narrative for the last time when he confronts Mirabella, the only character he encounters in the poem whose distress he cannot mitigate, partly, perhaps, because her story intersects with his own in various thematic and literal ways. Several fundamental aspects of Arthur's romantic quest for the Faery Queen converge in the figure and story of Mirabella, allowing the episode to serve as a summary analysis of some of the more problematical dimensions of the poem's unifying quest. Mirabella is accompanied and abused by Scorn and Disdain, her defining attributes and two of the most ubiquitous presences in Renaissance love poetry; she is the cold, proud, and therefore powerful mistress of the sonnets and of complaint poetry generally; in turn, she is the untouchable virgin, who preserves her autonomy and authority by resisting the sexual transgression of men, whose invasion of her would reduce her to their property. All this points unavoidably to her being a perverse type of Belphoebe, which is why Timias appears, only to be bound by Disdain (6.7.48-9) and led "like a dog" (6.8.5)—like the faithful, submissive pet who follows at Belphoebe's heels through Books 3 and 4.

If Timias links Mirabella to Belphoebe, then Arthur links her to Gloriana, which makes Arthur's encounter with Mirabella a disconcerting preview of his destined encounter with the mighty queen. Spenser renders the connection more likely than it might otherwise seem by bringing into conjunction Mirabella's story, Arthur's story of his youth in Wales, and Arthur's dream-vision of the Faery Queen. During his "freshest flowre of youthly yeares," Arthur tells Una, he "euer scornd" the "idle name of loue," laughing at lovers and "blow[ing] the fire, which them to ashes brent"; even "Their God himselfe, grieu'd at [his] libertie," could not entice him to love, though Cupid "Shot many a dart" (1.9.9-10). Similarly, "In prime of youthly yeares, when first the flowre / Of beauty gan to bud," Mirabella, "sitting . . . on the scorners stoole, / Did laugh at those that did lament and plaine," refusing to "leaue [her] loued libertie" (6.8.20-1; compare 6.7.28-30). Cupid, of course, catches them both in their vain desire to be free of love: Arthur falls in love with his vision of the Faery Queen (1.9.14-15), and Mirabella, while being abused by the embodiments of her own scorn and disdain, must wander until she saves as many loves as she had refused (6.7.37).

Considering the intimate relationship between the stories of Arthur and Mirabella, Arthur's meeting with Mirabella might subtly presage his reception by Gloriana; that is, just as Mirabella refuses to allow Arthur to kill Disdain because her life depends upon his remaining alive (see 6.8.17), so Gloriana must disdain Arthur's love in order to sustain her power. Students of the Elizabethan age, like the Elizabethans themselves, know that Elizabeth used her virgin status to enhance her autonomous power and that she played the disdainful mistress to keep her favorites submissive, which is exactly what Belphoebe does, Mirabella attempts to do, and Gloriana might well do. For although the Faery Queen who visits Arthur in his dream-vision represents one manifestation of Gloriana, it is difficult to imagine the queen who recalls Artegall from Ireland making "goodly glee and louely blandishment" to Arthur or any man (1.9.14). Mirabella's strategies seem rather more likely to serve the exigencies of a woman in power, whether Gloriana or Elizabeth, than those employed by the seductive creature who inhabits Arthur's dream. In contrast to Spenser's narrator, who argues that the "noblest" woman is the one served in love by the "noblest knight," Mirabella reasons that "the more she did all loue despize, / The more would wretched louers her adore"; and she knows that "her beautie had such soueraine might, / That with the onely twinckle of her eye, / She could or saue or spill, whom she would hight" (6.7.29-31). This "Ladie of her libertie" (6.7.31) may be the kind of woman Arthur is destined to meet in Cleopolis. Whatever the value of the foregoing radical conjectures, Arthur meets his match in Mirabella: she will not let him kill Disdain or free her from her torment, which makes his final enterprise, after triumphant victories throughout *The Faerie Queene*, something of a failure. Arthur goes "onward still / On his first quest" (6.8.30), but as the final Briton leaves the poem, Spenser may be suggesting that no apocalyptic marriage will take place in Cleopolis.

Sadness, longing, and relative failure dominate the Britons' entrances into and exits from the narrative of Faeryland. Redcrosse enters "too solemne sad" and Una "As one that inly mournd: so was she sad" (1.1.2,4); when last she appears, she has been "left to mourne" (1.12.41), and he leaves the poem perplexed, at best, by his disturbing conversation with Britomart concerning Artegall. When Artegall enters in person, disguised as the salvage knight and soon to be seeking murderous vengeance on Britomart, he seems perfectly capable of the outrageously unchivalric behavior of which Britomart accuses him. He exits the poem "halfe sad," no doubt pondering his relative failure in Ireland, his tarnished reputation, and his upcoming reprimand by Gloriana (6.1.4). Arthur and Britomart enter Faeryland in a state of romantic longing, and they leave the story in the same mood, Britomart in "anguish" over Artegall's absence (5.7.45) and Arthur, after failing to help Mirabella, "still" searching for the vision of his dream (6.8.30). The Britons move out of the narrative feeling troubled and world-weary.

Not so the Faery knights Guyon and Calidore, who seem incapable of feeling doubt, despair, longing, helplessness, or failure and constitutionally deficient in their ability to examine themselves and comprehend their inadequacies; although they occasionally feel mildly troubled or confused, they usually act with myopic self-confidence, exhibiting a general blindness to the consequences of their actions. These characteristics, while making them, in many ways, perfect civil servants, also make them, on occasion, somewhat shallow and foolish. Nonetheless, Guyon's destruction of the Bower of Bliss focuses and sets in motion the narrative of *The Faerie Queene*'s central books, and Calidore's intrusion into pastoral Faeryland influences decisively the poem's conclusion.

Like Artegall's aborted "reform" of Ireland, Guyon's demolition of the Bower of Bliss may exceed his assigned duty: to capture Acrasia and send her to Cleopolis. But it is quite a show, whether motivated by frustrated desire or merely by righteous anger. In a "tempest of . . . wrathfulness" and "with rigour pittilesse," the knight of temperance breaks, fells, defaces, spoils, suppresses, burns, and razes gardens, buildings, and all, "And of the fairest late, now made the fowlest place" (2.12.83). Guyon's action, although an appropriate climax of Book 2, also epitomizes a recurrent feature of Spenserian allegory: Guyon destroys a place representing, in part, illicit sexuality, but instead of diminishing the influence and prevalence of lust and erotic desire in the narrative, Guyon's action sets them loose to dominate it for much of the poem, particularly Books 3 and 4. Guyon's action also generates one of the primary questions for which the poem seeks answers: since erotic desire can be neither denied nor destroyed, and since, as Books 1 and 2 demonstrate, repressing it causes intractable problems, how might it best be controlled, legitimized, and accommodated?

The analysis of this question begins when Britomart effortlessly unhorses Guyon (from a borrowed horse?) at the beginning of Book 3, an action that illustrates the limitations of temperance and the broader capabilities of chastity in dealing with erotic desire. Finding himself on the ground behind his horse, Guyon gets up, "Full of disdainefull wrath," and grabs his sword, ready to attack Britomart. Warned by the Palmer that Britomart holds an "enchaunted speare" and pacified by Arthur, who blames Guyon's fall on a loose bridle, Guyon relents (3.1.9-11); but the fact remains that Guyon has difficulty controlling his anger and his horse. Following a formal allegorical "reconcilement" among Britomart, Guyon, and Arthur (3.1.12), the two men take off after Florimell "to win thereby / Most goodly meede, the fairest Dame aliue," an action that places the reconciliation of temperance and chastity in a potentially ironic context, especially considering that Britomart "Would not so lightly follow beauties chace" (3.1.18,19). Guyon disappears from the narrative until, amid the confusion following the wedding of Marinell and Florimell, he appears unexpectedly out of the crowd to claim his stolen horse from Braggadochio, who had just watched his snowy Florimell melt. The episode is slapstick comedy: Braggadochio refuses to give up the horse; Guyon is about to kill him and must be restrained by Artegall; two knights attempt to open the horse's mouth, where Guyon claims they will find a black, horseshoe-shaped birthmark that will prove the horse his; the horse breaks one's ribs and bites the other on the shoulder; Guyon talks to the horse, which recognizes his voice and allows him to display the birthmark; the horse jumps for joy, Guyon and the horse exit the poem, and readers smile (see 5.3.24-36).

Calidore's activities near the end of the poem are not so likely to raise a smile, or at least not a good-humored one, for his actions may be interpreted to precipitate the troubling dissolution of *The Faerie Queene*'s fictional world. When Calidore enters the pastoral world, the intricately woven fabric of Spenser's multiform fictional world begins to unravel. Calidore, in an ultimately tragic replay of Venus's search for Cupid (3.6.13-7), chases the Blatant Beast from court to cities to towns to farms and then "into the open fields"; finally, he "force[s] him to flie" into the sheepfolds and even "to the litle cots, where shepherds lie" (6.9.3-4). One day, coming upon some shepherds "Playing on pypes, and caroling apace" while their sheep feed, Calidore asks them if they have seen the beast "which he had thether brought" (6.9.5). They have not seen the Blatant Beast because, in essence, they cannot see it: their innocence, honesty, generosity, and true and simple courtesy blind them to it and make them immune to its sting. But Calidore knows it is among them; he has "brought" it into their world; and as the episode proceeds, Spenser makes clear the degree to which Calidore's manipulative and dissembling courtly version of courtesy implicates him in the work of the Beast and, thereby, in the destruction of the pastoral world and the dissolution of Colin Clout's imaginative vision.

During his stay in the pastoral world, Calidore is manipulative, crude, foolish, insincere, lustful, voyeuristic, dishonest, disruptive, and altogether discourteous. He shirks his duty to Gloriana by abandoning his quest; he takes advantage of Meliboe's generosity; he misinterprets Meliboe's subtle disquisition on the relationship between fate and self-fashioning because he is too busy leering at Pastorella; he stupidly offers Meliboe money; he patronizes Coridon; and, in an act that might be said to break the back of the poem, he vainly and tactlessly invades Colin Clout's imaginative vision, causing it to vanish and provoking Colin to break his pipe for the second time in his career. The invasion of the Brigants into the pastoral world, the closest equivalent to martial conquest in the Faeryland narrative, is analogous to and indirectly related to Calidore's—and the Blatant Beast's—invasion of the pastoral world and of Colin's vision. Since the Brigants inhabit an island, they invade Faeryland from outside its borders; with their intrusion, Spenser's carefully constructed boundary between Faeryland and the world outside begins to collapse, presaging its ultimate disintegration in the final stanzas of the poem.

Calidore rescues Pastorella from the Brigants, returns her to her parents, and, finally, subdues the Blatant Beast with "a muzzell strong" and "a great long chaine" (6.12.34). He proudly parades the Beast through Faeryland, where "all the people . . . did round about him throng . . . And much admyr'd the Beast, but more admyr'd the Knight" (6.12.37). The Beast remains chained until, "long after" Calidore's feat, "whether wicked fate so framed, / Or fault of men, he broke his yron chaine, / And got into the world at liberty againe" (6.12.38). Although Spenser's narrator blames fate or human error for the Beast's escape, the whole allegory of *The Faerie Queene* suggests a different and more troubling explanation. As the allegorical embodiment of social disorder—of the myriad unpleasant, injurious, and repellent products of human weakness that emerge from social exchange—the Blatant Beast cannot be silenced or tamed any more than error can always be avoided, lust finally quenched, or injustice quelled. Sometimes the Beast's bark and bite must simply be endured; at best, Spenser's poem teaches, the Beast's assault might be controlled or its injury minimized by confronting it with honesty, integrity, restraint, generosity, humility, circumspection, self-awareness, love, and courtesy. Perhaps the Hermit offers the best advice in concluding his instructions to the wounded Timias and Serena: "Shun secresie, and talke in open sight" (6.6.14).

At the end of *The Faerie Queene*, however, the Beast runs rampant, fracturing the boundaries of Spenser's fictional world. He breaks into "Britaine land," the sixth-century home of the Briton knights, where "none of [Arthur's knights] could euer bring him into band" (6.12.39). Finally, Spenser's meticulous anatomy of Tudor history collapses, not in the apocalyptic moment when time shall be no more, but in the moment when the Blatant Beast breaches the boundary between fiction and actuality, bursting out of the historical fiction into Elizabethan England. No one there "may him now restraine, / He growen is so great and strong of late"; in his attack, he spares neither "learned wits" nor "gentle Poets rime" (6.12.40).

In the final stanza, Spenser's narrator vanishes and the poet faces the Beast, sprung out of the fiction to haunt him. He begins with characteristic Spenserian mock humility and then becomes defensive: even "this homely verse," the "meanest" among his "many" poems, will not "escape [the Beast's] venemous despite" any more than his "former writs, all were they clearest / From blamefull blot"; the same "wicked tongues" that previously brought down upon his works, and therefore him, "a mighty Peres displeasure" will surely do the same once again (6.12.41). Spenser's attackers, including, presumably, the "Pere" Lord Burghley, whom Spenser here identifies with the Blatant Beast, comprise all those in his audience who find poetry useless and dangerous, at once a waste of time and morally and politically suspect. Readers have met these "Stoicke censours" (4.Proem.3) before: they are the same ones who would judge *The Faerie Queene* to be "th'aboundance of an idle braine" and "painted forgery, / Rather then matter of iust memory," merely because most of the narrative takes place in Faeryland, a realm they cannot find on a map (2.Proem.1); and they are those who, like the "rugged forhead" himself, "sharply wite" Spenser's "looser rimes . . . For praising loue . . . And magnifying louers deare debate," those "that cannot loue, / Ne in their frosen hearts feele kindly flame"—pitiable creatures, at best (4.Proem.1-2).

Spenser concludes the stanza and the poem with a bitterly ironic concession to the charges he predicts will be leveled at his poem by the contemporary embodiments of the Blatant Beast: "Therfore do you my rimes keep better measure, / And seeke to please, that now is counted wisemens threasure" (6.12.41). The irony lies in the ambiguity of the lines. Spenser himself does not concede to the implied demands of his abusers; rather, he requests the cooperation of his "rimes," over which, given the mercurial and unquantifiable influence of the muse, the poet has limited control. Even if his "rimes" do "seeke to please," they may not be any more successful than they have been in the past. While his detractors seem to be the ones his "rimes" should attempt to "please," Spenser's use of the word betrays his caginess, for *please* intimates another and much more complex interpretive context: the purpose and value of poetry. As every student of Elizabethan literature knows, Sidney argues in his *Defence* that poetry teaches virtue more successfully than history or philosophy because it delights its readers more than cold facts or abstract theories do—it pleases in order to instruct. Spenser, however, seems to be suggesting that his "rimes" should please rather than instruct, which is exactly what the "mighty Pere" would least desire them to do. The irony redoubles if readers consider some lines from Spenser's Letter to Ralegh. In the section of the Letter in which Spenser discusses his method of allegorical composition, he responds to those who, like Burghley and his cohorts, find his "Methode . . . displeasaunt" because they would "rather haue good discipline deliuered plainly in way of precepts . . . then thus clowdily enwrapped in Allegoricall deuises." Spenser tells them that they "should be satisfide with the vse of these dayes, seeing all things accounted by their showes, and nothing esteemed of, that is not delightfull and pleasing to commune sence." In other words, Spenser says he writes allegory rather than moral treatises because his duty as epic poet demands that he attract a national audience, an obligation he can accomplish only by serving the public "good discipline" dressed in pleasing "showes": "So much more profitable and gratious is doctrine by ensample, then by rule." Six years later, in the last line of his poem, Spenser asks his "rimes" either to abandon their national audience by pleasing their detractors or, even more cynically, to eschew their didactic obligation by offering mere entertainment, which, given the deteriorated state of the world, "now is counted wisemens threasure."

Spenser creates a multiform fictional universe capable of accommodating heroic epic, coordinating epic and romance quest structures, anatomizing Tudor history, and analyzing moral, social, and erotic existence. He writes what he calls in the Letter to Ralegh an allegorical historical fiction; in the conventional terminology he avoids, the poem turns out to be an epic without a war and a romance without a happy ending: a tragic romance of epic scope with lyric, comic, and pastoral accompaniments. At the end of Book 6, with all the main characters stranded in Faeryland, Spenser terminates his monumental creation by collapsing it into the reality of a contemporary Elizabethan world infected by the horrendous Blatant Beast.

Bibliography

Primary Sources

Adams, Hazard, ed. *Critical Theory Since Plato.* New York: Harcourt, Brace, Jovanovich, 1971.

Ariosto, Lodovico. *Orlando Furioso.* Trans. Sir John Harington. Ed. Graham Hough. Carbondale, IL: Southern Illinois Univ. Press, 1962.

———. *Orlando Furioso.* Trans. Guido Waldman. New York: Oxford Univ. Press, 1974.

Camden, William. *Britannia.* Trans. Richard Gough. 1806. Reprinted Hildesheim: Georg-olms Verlag, 1974.

Chaucer, Geoffrey. *The Complete Poetry and Prose of Geoffrey Chaucer.* Ed. John H. Fisher. New York: Holt, Rinehart and Winston, 1977.

French, Walter Hoyt and Charles Brockway Hale, eds. *Middle English Metrical Romances.* New York: Prentice-Hall, 1930.

Gibbs, A.C. *Middle English Romances.* Evanston, IL: Northwestern Univ. Press, 1966.

Gilbert, Allan H., ed. *Literary Criticism: Plato to Dryden.* New York: American Book, 1940.

Homer. *The Iliad.* Trans. Richard Lattimore. 1951. Reprinted, Chicago: Univ. of Chicago Press, 1970.

———. *The Odyssey.* Trans. Robert Fitzgerald. 1961. Reprinted, Garden City, NY: Doubleday, 1963.

Lorris, Guillaume de and Jean de Meun. *The Romance of the Rose.* Trans. Harry W. Robbins. Ed. Charles W. Dunn. New York: Dutton, 1962.

Malory, Sir Thomas. *Works*. Ed. Eugene Vinaver. New York: Oxford Univ. Press, 1977.

Ovid. *Metamorphoses*. Trans. Rolfe Humphries. 1955. Reprinted, Bloomington, IN: Univ. of Indiana Press, 1972.

Rumble, Thomas C., ed. *The Breton Lays in Middle English*. Detroit: Wayne State Univ. Press, 1965.

Sands, Donald B., ed. *Middle English Verse Romances*. New York: Holt, Rinehart and Winston, 1966.

Schmidt, A.V.C. and Nicolas Jacobs, eds. *Medieval English Romances*. 2 parts. London: Hodder and Stoughton, 1980.

Sidney, Sir Philip. *Miscellaneous Prose of Sir Philip Sidney*. Ed. Katherine Duncan-Jones and Jan Van Dorsten. Oxford: Clarendon Press, 1973.

———. *The Countess of Pembroke's Arcadia* (The Old Arcadia). Ed. Jean Robertson. Oxford: Clarendon Press, 1973.

Spenser, Edmund. *The Complete Poetical Works of Edmund Spenser*. Ed. R.E. Neil Dodge. New York: Houghton Mifflin, 1908.

———. *The Works of Edmund Spenser: A Variorum Edition*. Ed. Edwin Greenlaw et al. 10 vols. Baltimore: Johns Hopkins Press. 1932–57.

———. *The Faerie Queene*. Ed. A.C. Hamilton. New York: Longman, 1977.

———. *The Yale Edition of the Shorter Poems of Edmund Spenser*. Ed. William Oram et al. New Haven: Yale Univ. Press, 1989.

Tasso, Torquato. *Discourses on the Heroic Poem*. Trans. Mariella Cavalchini and Irene Samuel. Oxford: Clarendon Press, 1973.

———. *Jerusalem Delivered*. Trans. Edward Fairfax. Carbondale, IL: Southern Illinois Univ. Press, 1962.

Tolkein, J.R.R. and E.V. Gordon, eds. *Sir Gawain and the Green Knight*. 2nd ed., rev. by Norman Davis. Oxford: Clarendon Press, 1967.

Troyes, Chrétien de. *Arthurian Romances*. Trans. W.W. Comfort. London: J.M. Dent, 1967.

Virgil. *The Aeneid*. Trans. Frank O. Copley. 2nd ed. Indianapolis, IN: Bobbs-Merrill, 1975.

Secondary Sources

Alpers, Paul J. *The Poetry of The Faerie Queene*. Princeton: Princeton Univ. Press, 1967.

Anderson, Judith H. *The Growth of a Personal Voice. Piers Plowman and The Faerie Queene*. New Haven: Yale Univ. Press, 1976.

———. "'Myn auctour': Spenser's Enabling Fiction and Eumnestes' 'immortal scrine.'" In *Unfolded Tales: Essays on Renaissance Romance*, ed. George M. Logan and Gordon Teskey, 16–31. Ithaca, NY: Cornell Univ. Press, 1989.

Andersson, Theodore M. *Early Epic Scenery: Homer, Virgil, and the Medieval Legacy*. Ithaca, NY: Cornell Univ. Press, 1976.

Arthos, John. *On the Poetry of Spenser and the Form of Romances*. London: George Allen and Unwin, 1956.

Auerbach, Erich. *Mimesis: The Representation of Reality in Western Literature*. Trans. Willard Trask. Princeton: Princeton Univ. Press, 1953.

Baker, Herschel, ed. *Four Essays on Romance*. Cambridge: Harvard Univ. Press, 1971.

Barker, Francis, Peter Hulme, and Margaret Iverson, eds. *Uses of History: Marxism, Postmodernism, and the Renaissance*. Manchester: Manchester Univ. Press, 1991.

Barney, Stephen A. *Allegories of History, Allegories of Love*. Hamden, CT: Archon, 1979.

Beer, Gillian. *Romance*. London: Metheun, 1970.

Bender, John B. *Spenser and Literary Pictorialism*. Princeton: Princeton Univ. Press, 1972.

Bennett, H.S. *Chaucer and the Fifteenth Century*. Oxford: Clarendon Press, 1947.

Bennett, J.A.W., ed., *Essays on Malory*. Oxford: Clarendon Press, 1963.

———. "Genre, Milieu, and the 'Epic-Romance.'" In *English Institute Essays, 1951*, ed. Alan S. Downer, 95–125. New York: Columbia Univ. Press, 1952. Reprinted, New York: AMS Press, 1965.

Bennett, Josephine Waters. *The Evolution of* The Faerie Queene. 1942. Reprinted, New York: Burt Franklin, 1960.

Berger, Harry, Jr. *The Allegorical Temper: Vision and Reality in Book II of Spenser's* Faerie Queene. New Haven: Yale Univ. Press, 1957.

———. "Spenser's Gardens of Adonis: Force and Form in the Renaissance Imagination." *Univ. of Toronto Quarterly* 30 (1960–61): 128–49.

———. "The Prospect of Imagination: Spenser and the Limits of Poetry." *Studies in English Literature* 1 (1961): 93–120.

———. "A Secret Discipline: *The Faerie Queene*, Book VI." In *Form and Convention in the Poetry of Edmund Spenser: Selected Essays from the English Institute*, ed. William Nelson, 35–75. New York: Columbia Univ. Press, 1963.

———. "The Renaissance Imagination: Second World and Green World." *Centennial Review* 9 (1965): 36–78.

———. Introduction to *Spenser: A Collection of Critical Essays*, ed. Harry Berger, Jr., 1–12. Englewood Cliffs, NJ: Prentice-Hall, 1968.

———. "The *Mutabilitie Cantos*: Archaism and Evolution in Retrospect." In *Spenser: A Collection of Critical Essays*, ed. Harry Berger, Jr., 146–76. Englewood Cliffs, NJ: Prentice-Hall, 1968.

———. "The Spenserian Dynamics." *Studies in English Literature* 8 (1968): 1–18.

———. "The Structure of Merlin's Chronicle in *The Faerie Queene III (iii)*." *Studies in English Literature* 9 (1969): 39–51.

———. *Revisionary Play: Studies in the Spenserian Dynamics*. Berkeley: Univ. of California Press, 1988.

———. "'Kidnapped Romance': Discourse in *The Faerie Queene*." In *Unfolded Tales: Essays on Renaissance Romance*, ed. George M. Logan and Gordon Teskey, 208–56. Ithaca, NY: Cornell Univ. Press, 1989.

Berry, Philippa. *Of Chastity and Power: Elizabethan Literature and the Unmarried Queen*. London: Routledge, 1989.

Berthoff, Warner. "Fiction, History, Myth: Notes Toward the Discrimination of Narrative Forms." In *The Interpretation of Narrative: Theory and Practice*, ed. Morton W. Bloomfield, 263–86. Cambridge: Harvard Univ. Press, 1970.

Bogdanow, Fanni. *The Romance of the Grail: A Study of the Structure and Genesis of a Thirteenth-Century Arthurian Prose Romance*. New York: Barnes and Noble, 1966.

Bono, Barbara J. *Literary Transvaluation: From Vergilian Epic to Shakespearean Tragicomedy*. Berkeley: Univ. of California Press, 1984.

Bowra, C.M. *From Virgil to Milton*. London: MacMillan, 1948.

Brandt, William J. *The Shape of Medieval History: Studies in Modes of Perception*. New Haven: Yale Univ. Press, 1966.

Burkhart, Robert E. "History, the Epic, and *The Faerie Queene*." *English Studies* 56 (1975): 14–19.

Burns, Norman T. and Christopher J. Reagan, eds. *Concepts of the Hero in the Middle Ages and the Renaissance*. Albany, NY: State Univ. of New York Press, 1975.

Burrow, Colin. *Epic Romance: Homer to Milton*. Oxford: Clarendon Press, 1993.

Butterfield, H. *The Statecraft of Machiavelli*. New York: Macmillan, 1956.

Cain, Thomas H. *Praise in* The Faerie Queene. Lincoln, NE: Univ. of Nebraska Press, 1978.

Calin, William. *The Epic Quest: Studies in Four Old French Chansons de Geste*. Baltimore: Johns Hopkins Press, 1966.

Campbell, Joseph. *The Hero with a Thousand Faces*. 1956. Reprinted, Cleveland: World Publishing, 1967.

Carruth, Hayden. "Spenser and His Modern Critics." *Hudson Review* 22 (1969): 139–47.

Cheney, Donald. *Spenser's Image of Nature: Wild Man and Shepherd in* The Faerie Queene. New Haven: Yale Univ. Press, 1966.

Colie, Rosalie L. *The Resources of Kind: Genre-Theory in the Renaissance*. Ed. Barbara K. Lewalski. Berkeley: Univ. of California Press, 1973.

Cook, Albert. *The Classic Line: A Study in Epic Poetry*. Bloomington, IN: Indiana Univ. Press, 1966.

Craig, Joanne. "The Image of Mortality: Myth and History in *The Faerie Queene*." *ELH* 39 (1972): 520–44.

Curtius, Ernst Robert. *European Literature in the Latin Middle Ages*. Trans. Willard Trask. 1953. Reprinted, London: Routledge, 1979.

Cuthbertson, Gilbert Morris. *Political Myth and Epic*. Lansing, MI: Michigan State Univ. Press, 1975.

Damon, Phillip. "History and Idea in Renaissance Criticism." In *Literary Criticism and Historical Understanding: Selected Papers of the English Institute*, ed. Phillip Damon, 25–51. New York: Columbia Univ. Press, 1967.

Davis, B.E.C. *Edmund Spenser: A Critical Study*. 1933. Reprinted, New York: Russell and Russell, 1962.

Davis, Walter R. *Idea and Act in Elizabethan Fiction*. Princeton: Princeton Univ. Press. 1969.

Deneef, A. Leigh. *Spenser and the Motives of Metaphor*. Durham, NC: Duke Univ. Press, 1982.

Dobin, Howard. *Merlin's Disciples: Prophecy, Poetry, and Power in Renaissance England*. Stanford, CA: Stanford Univ. Press, 1990.

Dollimore, Jonathan. *Radical Tragedy: Religion, Ideology, and Power in the Drama of Shakespeare and His Contemporaries*. Chicago: Univ. of Chicago Press, 1984.

———. Introduction to *Political Shakespeare: New Essays in Cultural Materialism*, ed. Jonathan Dollimore and Alan Sinfield, 2–17. Ithaca, NY: Cornell Univ. Press, 1985.

Dubrow, Heather and Richard Strier. Introduction to *The Historical Renaissance: New Essays on Tudor and Stuart Literature and Culture*, ed. Heather Dubrow and Richard Strier, 1–12. Chicago: Univ. of Chicago Press, 1988.

Dundas, Judith. *The Spider and the Bee: The Artistry of Spenser's* Faerie Queene. Urbana, IL: Univ. of Illinois Press, 1985.

Dunseath, T.K. *Spenser's Allegory of Justice in Book Five of* The Faerie Queene. Princeton: Princeton Univ. Press, 1968.

Durling, Robert M. *The Figure of the Poet in Renaissance Epic*. Cambridge, MA: Harvard Univ. Press, 1965.

Evans, Maurice. *Spenser's Anatomy of Heroism: A Commentary on* The Faerie Queene. Cambridge: Cambridge Univ. Press, 1970.

Felperin, Howard. "Romance and Romanticism." *Critical Inquiry* 6 (1980): 691–706.

Ferguson, Arthur B. *Clio Unbound: Perception of the Social and Cultural Past in Renaissance England*. Durham, NC: Duke Univ. Press, 1979.

Ferguson, Margaret W. *Trials of Desire: Renaissance Defenses of Poetry*. New Haven: Yale Univ. Press, 1983.

Fichter, Andrew. *Poets Historical: Dynastic Epic in the Renaissance*. New Haven: Yale Univ. Press, 1982.

Fletcher, Angus. *Allegory: The Theory of a Symbolic Mode*. Ithaca, NY: Cornell Univ. Press, 1964.

———. *The Prophetic Moment: An Essay on Spenser*. Chicago: Univ. of Chicago Press, 1971.

Fowler, Alastair. *Kinds of Literature: An Introduction to the Theory of Genres and Modes*. Cambridge: Harvard Univ. Press, 1982.

Frye, Northrop. *Anatomy of Criticism: Four Essays*. Princeton: Princeton Univ. Press, 1957.

———. "Structure of Imagery in *The Faerie Queene*." *Univ. of Toronto Quarterly* 30 (1960–61): 109–27.

———. *A Study of English Romanticism*. New York: Random House, 1968.

Frye, Susan. *Elizabeth I: The Competition for Representation*. New York: Oxford Univ. Press, 1993.

Fussner, F. Smith. *The Historical Revolution: English Historical Writing and Thought 1580–1640*. New York: Columbia Univ. Press, 1962.

———. *Tudor History and the Historians*. New York: Basic Books, 1970.

Gardner, Fdmund G. *The Arthurian Legend in Italian Literature*. New York: Dutton, 1930.

Giamatti, A. Bartlett. *The Earthly Paradise and the Renaissance Epic.* Princeton: Princeton Univ. Press, 1966.

Goldberg, Jonathan. *Endlesse Worke: Spenser and the Structures of Discourse.* Baltimore: Johns Hopkins Univ. Press, 1981.

———. "The Poet's Authority: Spenser, Jonson, and James VI and I." In *The Power of Forms in the English Renaissance*, ed. Stephen Greenblatt, 81–99. Norman, OK: Pilgrim, 1982.

———. "The Politics of Renaissance Literature: A Review Essay." *ELH* 49 (1982): 514–42.

———. *James I and the Politics of Literature: Jonson, Shakespeare, Donne, and Their Contemporaries.* Baltimore: Johns Hopkins Univ. Press, 1983.

Gradon, Pamela. *Form and Style in Early English Literature.* London: Methuen, 1971.

Greenblatt, Stephen. *Renaissance Self-Fashioning: From More to Shakespeare.* Chicago: Univ. of Chicago Press, 1980.

———. Introduction to *The Power of Forms in the English Renaissance*, ed. Stephen Greenblatt, 3–6. Norman, OK: Pilgrim, 1982.

———. *Shakespearean Negotiations: The Circulation of Social Energy in Renaissance England.* Berkeley: Univ. of California Press, 1988.

———. Introduction to *Learning to Curse: Essays in Early Modern Culture*, 1–15. New York: Routledge, 1990.

———. "Kindly Visions." *New Yorker*, 11 October 1993, 112–20.

Greene, Thomas. "The Norms of Epic." *Comparative Literature* 13 (1961): 193–207.

———. *The Descent From Heaven: A Study in Epic Continuity.* New Haven: Yale Univ. Press, 1963.

———. "The Flexibility of the Self in Renaissance Literature." In *The Disciplines of Criticism: Essays in Literary Theory, Interpretation, and History*, ed. Peter Demetz, Thomas Greene, and Lowrey Nelson, Jr., 241–64. New Haven: Yale Univ. Press, 1968.

Greenlaw, Edwin. "Spenser's Fairy Mythology." *Studies in Philology* 15 (1918): 105–22.

———. *Studies in Spenser's Historical Allegory.* Johns Hopkins Monographs in Literary History 2. 1932. Reprinted, New York: Octagon Books, 1967.

Gross, Kenneth. *Spenserian Poetics: Idolatry, Iconoclasm, and Magic.* Ithaca, NY: Cornell Univ. Press, 1985.

Guillory, John. *Poetic Authority: Spenser, Milton, and Literary History.* New York: Columbia Univ. Press, 1983.

Hamilton, A.C. *The Structure of Allegory in* The Faerie Queene. Oxford: Clarendon Press, 1961.

Hankins, John Erskine. *Source and Meaning in Spenser's Allegory: A Study of* The Faerie Queene. Oxford: Clarendon Press, 1971.

Hanning, Robert W. *The Individual in Twelfth-Century Romance.* New Haven: Yale Univ. Press,1977.

Hathaway, Baxter. *The Age of Criticism: The Late Renaissance in Italy.* Ithaca, NY: Cornell Univ. Press, 1962.

———. *Marvels and Commonplaces: Renaissance Literary Criticism.* New York: Random House, 1968.

Hays, Denys. *Annalists and Historians: Western Historiography from the Eighth to the Eighteenth Centuries.* London: Metheun, 1977.

Helgerson, Richard. *The Elizabethan Prodigals.* Berkeley: Univ. of California Press, 1976.

———. "The New Poet Presents Himself: Spenser and the Idea of a Literary Career." *PMLA* 93 (1978): 893–911.

———. "The Elizabethan Laureate: Self-Presentation and the Literary System." *ELH* 46 (1979): 193–220.

———. "Inventing Noplace, or the Power of Negative Thinking." In *The Power of Forms in the English Renaissance*, ed. Stephen Greenblatt, 101–21. Norman, OK: Pilgrim, 1982.

———. *Self-Crowned Laureates: Spenser, Jonson, Milton, and the Literary System.* Berkeley: Univ. of California Press, 1983.

———. *Forms of Nationhood: The Elizabethan Writing of England.* Chicago: Univ. of Chicago Press, 1992.

Herendeen, Wyman H. "Wanton Discourse and the Engines of Time: William Camden—Historian among Poets-Historical." In *Renaissance Rereadings: Intertext and Context*, ed. Maryanne Cline Horowitz, Anne J. Cruz, and Wendy A. Furman, 142–56. Urbana, IL: Univ. of Illinois Press, 1988.

Hieatt, A. Kent. *Chaucer, Spenser, Milton: Mythopoeic Continuities and Transformations.* Montreal: McGill-Queen's Univ. Press, 1975.

———. "The Projected Continuation of *The Faerie Queene*: *Rome Delivered*?" *Spenser Studies* 8 (1990): 335–42.

Hill, D.M. "Romance as Epic." *English Studies* 44 (1963): 95–107.

Hollister, C. Warren, ed. *The Twelfth-Century Renaissance.* New York: John Wiley and Sons, 1969.

Honig, Edwin. *Dark Conceit: The Making of Allegory.* Evanston, IL: Northwestern Univ. Press, 1959.

Horton, Ronald Arthur. *The Unity of* The Faerie Queene. Athens, GA: Univ. of Georgia Press, 1978.

Hough, Graham. *A Preface to* The Faerie Queene. New York: Norton, 1962.

Howard, Jean E. "The New Historicism in Renaissance Studies." *English Literary Renaissance* 16 (1986): 13–43.

Howard, Jean and Marion O'Conner, eds. *Shakespeare Reproduced.* New York: Methuen, 1987.

Hughes, Merritt Y. *Virgil and Spenser.* Univ. of California Publications in English. Vol. 2, No. 3. Berkeley: Univ. of California Press, 1929.

Hume, Anthea. *Edmund Spenser: Protestant Poet.* Cambridge: Cambridge Univ. Press, 1984.

Hurd, Richard. *Letters on Chivalry and Romance with the Third Elizabethan Dialogue.* Ed. Edith J. Morley. London: Henry Frowde, 1911.

Javitch, Daniel. *Poetry and Courtliness in Renaissance England.* Princeton: Princeton Univ. Press, 1978.

———. *Proclaiming a Classic: The Canonization of* Orlando Furioso. Princeton: Princeton Univ. Press, 1991.

Kane, George. *Middle English Literature: A Critical Study of the Romances, the Religious Lyrics,* Piers Plowman. London: Methuen, 1951.

Kaske, Carol V. "Spenser's Pluralistic Universe: The View from the Mount of Contemplation (*F.Q.* Ix)." In *Contemporary Thought on Edmund Spenser*, ed. Richard C. Frushell and Bernard J. Vondersmith, 121–49. Carbondale, IL: Southern Illinois Univ. Press, 1975.

Kelley, Donald R. "Elizabethan Political Thought." In *The Varieties of British Political Thought, 1500–1800*, ed. J.G.A. Pocock, 47–79. Cambridge: Cambridge Univ. Press, 1993.

Kendrick, T.D. *British Antiquity.* London: Methuen, 1950.

Ker, W.P. *Epic and Romance: Essays on Medieval Literature.* 1896. Reprinted, New York: Dover, 1957.

Kermode, Frank. *The Sense of an Ending: Studies in the Theory of Fiction.* New York: Oxford Univ. Press, 1967.

———. *Shakespeare, Spenser, Donne: Renaissance Essays.* New York: Viking, 1971.

King, John N. *Spenser's Poetry and the Reformation Tradition.* Princeton: Princeton Univ. Press, 1990.

Krier, Theresa M. *Gazing on Secret Sights: Spenser, Classical Imitation, and the Decorums of Vision.* Ithaca, NY: Cornell Univ. Press, 1990.

Leslie, Michael. *Spenser's "Fierce Warres and Faithfull Loves": Martial and Chivalric Symbolism in* The Faerie Queene. Totowa, NJ: Barnes and Noble, 1983.

Levin, Harry. "What is Realism?" In *Contexts of Criticism*, 67–75. Cambridge: Harvard Univ. Press, 1958.

Levine, Joseph M. *Humanism and History: Origins of Modern English Historiography*. Ithaca, NY: Cornell Univ. Press, 1987.

Levy, F.J. *Tudor Historical Thought*. San Marino, CA: Huntington Library, 1967.

Lewis, C.S. *The Allegory of Love: A Study in Medieval Tradition*. 1936. Reprinted, New York: Oxford Univ. Press, 1963.

———. *A Preface to* Paradise Lost. New York: Oxford Univ. Press, 1961.

———. *Studies in Medieval and Renaissance Literature*. Cambridge: Cambridge Univ. Press, 1966.

———. *Spenser's Images of Life*. Cambridge: Cambridge Univ. Press, 1967.

———. *English Literature in the Sixteenth Century, Excluding Drama*. 1954. Reprinted, Oxford: Clarendon Press, 1968.

Lincoln, Eleanor Terry, ed. *Pastoral and Romance: Modern Essays in Criticism*. Englewood Cliffs, NJ: Prentice-Hall, 1969.

MacCaffrey, Isabel G. *Spenser's Allegory: The Anatomy of Imagination*. Princeton: Princeton Univ. Press, 1976.

Manley, Lawrence. *Convention: 1500–1750*. Cambridge: Harvard Univ. Press, 1980.

———. "From Matron to Monster: Tudor-Stuart London and the Languages of Urban Description." In *The Historical Renaissance: New Essays on Tudor and Stuart Literature and Culture*, ed. Heather Dubrow and Richard Strier, 347–74. Chicago: Univ. of Chicago Press, 1988.

Maresca, Thomas E. *Three English Epics: Studies of* Troilus and Criseyde, The Faerie Queene, *and* Paradise Lost. Lincoln, NE: Univ. of Nebraska Press, 1979.

Marsh, Robert. "Historical Interpretation and the History of Criticism." In *Literary Criticism and Historical Understanding: Selected Papers of the English Institute*, ed. Phillip Damon, 1–24. New York: Columbia Univ. Press, 1967.

McCabe, Richard A. *The Pillars of Eternity: Time and Providence in* The Faerie Queene. Blackrock, Ireland: Irish Academic Press, 1989.

McCoy, Richard C. *The Rites of Knighthood: The Literature and Politics of Elizabethan Chivalry*. Berkeley: Univ. of California Press, 1989.

McKisack, Mary. *Medieval History in the Tudor Age*. Oxford: Clarendon Press, 1971.

Mehl, Dieter. *The Middle English Romances of the Thirteenth and Fourteenth Centuries*. New York: Barnes and Noble, 1969.

Miller, David Lee. *The Poem's Two Bodies: The Poetics of the 1590* Faerie Queene. Princeton: Princeton Univ. Press, 1988.

Miller, Jacqueline T. *Poetic License: Authority and Authorship in Medieval and Renaissance Contexts*. New York: Oxford Univ. Press, 1986.

Millican, Charles Bowie. *Spenser and the Table Round: A Study of the Contemporaneous Background for Spenser's Use of the Arthurian Legend*. Harvard Studies in Comparative Literature VIII. Cambridge: Harvard Univ. Press, 1932.

Montrose, Louis Adrian. "The Elizabethan Subject and the Spenserian Text." In *Literary Theory/Renaissance Texts*, ed. Patricia Parker and David Quint, 303–40. Baltimore: Johns Hopkins Univ. Press, 1986.

———. "Renaissance Literary Studies and the Subject of History." *English Literary Renaissance* 16 (1986): 5–12.

Moorman, Charles. *A Knyght There Was: The Evolution of the Knight in Literature*. Lexington, KY: Univ. of Kentucky Press, 1967.

Murrin, Michael. *The Veil of Allegory: Some Notes toward a Theory of Allegorical Rhetoric in the English Renaissance*. Chicago: Univ. of Chicago Press, 1969.

———. "The Rhetoric of Fairyland." In *The Rhetoric of Renaissance Poetry: From Wyatt to Milton*, ed. Thomas O. Sloan and Raymond B. Waddington, 73–95. Berkeley: Univ. of California Press, 1974.

———. *The Allegorical Epic: Essays in Its Rise and Decline*. Chicago: Univ. of Chicago Press, 1980.

Nagel, George H. "Philosophy of History before Historicism." *History and Theory* 3 (1964): 291–315.

Nelson, William. *The Poetry of Edmund Spenser: A Study*. New York: Columbia Univ. Press, 1963.

———. *Fact or Fiction: The Dilemma of the Renaissance Storyteller*. Cambridge: Harvard Univ. Press, 1973.

Nohrnberg, James. *The Analogy of* The Faerie Queene. Princeton: Princeton Univ. Press, 1976.

Norbrook, David. *Poetry and Politics in the English Renaissance*. London: Routledge, 1984.

O'Connell, Michael. *Mirror and Veil: The Historical Dimension of Spenser's* Faerie Queene. Chapel Hill, NC: Univ. of North Carolina Press, 1977.

Olson, Elder. *Aristotle's "Poetics" and English Literature: A Collection of Critical Essays*. New York: Columbia Univ. Press, 1963.

Orgel, Stephen. "Making Greatness Familiar." In *The Power of Forms in the English Renaissance*, ed. Stephen Greenblatt, 41–8. Norman, OK: Pilgrim, 1982.

Osgood, Charles Grosvenor. *A Concordance to the Poems of Edmund Spenser*. The Carnegie Institution of Washington, 1915.

Parker, M. Pauline. *The Allegory of* The Faerie Queene. Oxford: Clarendon Press, 1960.

Parker, Patricia A. *Inescapable Romance: Studies in the Poetics of a Mode.* Princeton: Princeton Univ. Press, 1979.

———. *Literary Fat Ladies: Rhetoric, Gender, and Property.* London: Methuen, 1987.

Patch, Howard Rollin. *The Other World, According to Descriptions in Medieval Literature.* Cambridge: Harvard Univ. Press, 1950.

Patterson, Lee. *Chaucer and the Subject of History.* Madison, WI: Univ. of Wisconsin Press, 1991.

Pechter, Edward. "The New Historicism and Its Discontents: Politicizing Renaissance Drama." *PMLA* 102 (1987): 292–303.

Piehler, Paul. *The Visionary Landscape: A Study in Medieval Allegory.* Montreal: McGill-Queen's Univ. Press, 1971.

Pocock, J.G.A. "The Sense of History in Renaissance England." In *William Shakespeare: His World, His Works, His Influence*, ed. John F. Andrews, vol. 1, 143–57. New York: Scribners, 1985.

Provost, Foster. "Treatments of Theme and Allegory in Twentieth-Century Criticism of *The Faerie Queene.*" In *Contemporary Thought on Edmund Spenser*, ed. Richard C. Frushell and Bernard J. Vondersmith, 1–40. Carbondale, IL: Southern Illinois Univ. Press, 1975.

Quilligan, Maureen. *Milton's Spenser: The Politics of Reading.* Ithaca, NY: Cornell Univ. Press, 1983.

Quint, David. *Origin and Originality in Renaissance Literature: Versions of the Source.* New Haven: Yale Univ. Press, 1983.

Rajan, Balachandra. "Closure." In *The Spenser Encyclopedia*, ed. A.C. Hamilton et al., 169–70. Toronto: Univ. of Toronto Press, 1990.

Rambus, Richard. *Spenser's Secret Career.* Cambridge: Cambridge Univ. Press, 1993.

Rathborne, Isabel E. *The Meaning of Spenser's Fairyland.* New York: Columbia Univ. Press, 1937.

Renwick, W.L. *Edmund Spenser: An Essay on Renaissance Literature.* 1925. Reprinted, London: Edward Arnold, 1961.

Roche, Thomas P., Jr. *The Kindly Flame: A Study of the Third and Fourth Books of Spenser's* Faerie Queene. Princeton: Princeton Univ. Press, 1964.

Sale, Roger. *Reading Spenser: An Introduction to* The Faerie Queene. New York: Random House, 1968.

Scholes, Robert and Robert Kellogg. *The Nature of Narrative.* New York: Oxford Univ. Press, 1966.

Sinfield, Alan. "Power and Ideology: An Outline Theory and Sidney's *Arcadia.*" *ELH* 52 (1985): 259–77.

Southern, R.W. *The Making of the Middle Ages*. New Haven: Yale Univ. Press, 1953.

Spens, Janet. *Spenser's* Faerie Queene*: An Interpretation*. New York: Russell and Russell, 1934.

Spingarn, Joel E. *A History of Literary Criticism in the Renaissance*. 1899. Reprinted, New York: Columbia Univ. Press, 1920.

Steadman, John M. *Milton and the Renaissance Hero*. Oxford: Oxford Univ. Press, 1967.

———. "The Arming of an Archetype: Heroic Virtue and the Conventions of Literary Epic." In *Concepts of the Hero in the Middle Ages and the Renaissance*, ed. Norman T. Burns and Christopher J. Reagan, 147–90. Albany, NY: State Univ. of New York Press, 1975.

Stevens, John. *Medieval Romance: Themes and Approaches*. London: Hutchinson Univ. Library, 1976.

Suzuki, Mihoko. *Metamorphoses of Helen: Authority, Difference, and the Epic*. Ithaca, NY: Cornell Univ. Press, 1989.

Teskey, Gordon. Introduction to *Unfolded Tales: Essays on Renaissance Romance*, ed. George M. Logan and Gordon Teskey, 1–15. Ithaca, NY: Cornell Univ. Press, 1989.

———. "Allegory." In *The Spenser Encyclopedia*, ed. A.C. Hamilton et al., 16–22. Toronto: Univ. of Toronto Press, 1990.

———. "Irony, Allegory, and Metaphysical Decay." *PMLA* 109 (1994): 397–408.

Tillyard, E.M.W. *The Elizabethan World Picture: A Study of the Idea of Order in the Age of Shakespeare, Donne, and Milton*. 1943. Reprinted, London: Chatto and Windus, 1973.

———. *The English Epic and Its Background.* 1954. Reprinted, Westport, CT: Greenwood Press, 1976.

Tonkin, Humphrey. *Spenser's Courteous Pastoral: Book Six of* The Faerie Queene. Oxford: Clarendon Press, 1972.

Tuve, Rosemond. *Allegorical Imagery: Some Medieval Books and Their Posterity*. Princeton: Princeton Univ. Press, 1966.

Vesser, H. Aram, ed. *The New Historicism*. New York: Routledge, 1988.

Vinaver, Eugene. *Malory*. Oxford: Oxford Univ. Press, 1929.

———. *The Rise of Romance*. Oxford: Clarendon Press, 1971.

Waller, Gary. *English Poetry of the Sixteenth Century*. London: Longman, 1986.

Waswo, Richard. *Language and Meaning in the Renaissance*. Princeton: Princcton Univ. Press, 1987.

Webb, William Stanford. "Vergil in Spenser's Epic Theory." *ELH* 4 (1937): 62–84.

Weinberg, Bernard. *A History of Literary Criticism in the Italian Renaissance.* 2 vols. Chicago: Univ. of Chicago Press, 1961.

Wells, Robin Headlam. *Spenser's* Faerie Queene *and the Cult of Elizabeth.* Totowa, NJ: Barnes and Noble, 1983.

Williams, Kathleen. *Spenser's World of Glass: A Reading of* The Faerie Queene. Berkeley: Univ. of California Press, 1966.

Willson, Elizabeth. *The Middle English Legends of Visits to the Other World and Their Relation to the Metrical Romances.* Diss. Private ed., distributed by Univ. of Chicago Libraries, 1917.

Wittig, Susan. *Stylistic and Narrative Structures in the Middle English Romances.* Austin, TX: Univ. of Texas Press, 1978.

Woolf, D.R. *The Idea of History in Early Stuart England: Erudition, Ideology, and "The Light of Truth" from the Accession of James I to the Civil War.* Toronto: Univ. of Toronto Press, 1990.

Yates, Frances A. *Astraea: The Imperial Theme in the Sixteenth Century.* London: Routledge, 1975.

Index

Abelard, Peter, 46–7
Abrams, Meyer, 82 n.11
Achilles, 20, 22, 34 n.4, 46
Acrasia, 15 n.10, 85 n.31, 96, 125
Adam, 53 n.9, 67, 69
Adam (and Eve), king (and queen) of Eden lands, 68–9, 77, 85 n.34, 96, 120–1
Aeneas, 4, 6, 7, 22, 44–6, 53 nn.9 and 12, 88, 95, 108, 114 n.30, 116 n.42
Aeneid. *See* Virgil
Aesculapius, 66
Africa, 69
Agamemnon, 53 n.11
Agape, 66
Agramante, 42
Albany. *See* Pictland
Alberti, Leone Battista, 82 n.10
Alcina, 43
Allen, Don Cameron, 54 n.13
Alma (and castle of), 5, 64, 66, 71, 75
Alpers, Paul, 12
Amazons, land of. *See* Radigund
America. *See* India
Amoret, 67, 102
Anchises, 7
Anderson, Judith H., 56 n.20
Angela, 71, 110
Angelica, 43
Antiquitie of Faerie lond, 92–3, 113 n.18
Apollo, 5, 66
Archimago, 65, 77, 120–1
Argonautica, 36 n.14
Ariosto, Lodovico, 4, 7, 11, 19, 21–2, 23, 30, 33, 34 n.5, 41–5, 51 nn.1, 3, and 4, 52 n.7, 79–80, 108–9, 116 n.42, 117 n.47
Aristotle (*Poetics*), 21–3, 35 n.12
Arlo hill, 68
Armada, 79
Artegall, 6, 29, 50, 53 n.9, 55 n.18, 69–70, 71–3, 75, 79, 87–8, 95–112, 117 n.48, 119–23, 125, 126
Arthos, John, 51 n.1
Arthur, 4, 6, 7, 13, 19, 24–30, 37 n.22, 38 n.28, 42, 48–50, 55 n.18, 61, 69, 71–3, 75, 79, 87–8, 90, 93, 95, 99–100, 105–12, 117 nn.45 and 46, 119–20, 123–6, 128
Astraea (Virgo), 5, 66, 69, 72, 75
Ate, cave of, 5, 64
Atlante, 43
Auerbach, Erich, 48–9, 56 n.23
Augustan line, 7, 108
Bacon, Francis, 28–9, 38 n.31
Barker, Francis, 16 n.14
Barney, Stephen A., 14 n.6
Belgard, Castle of, 113 n.8
Belgium (land of Belge), 6, 68, 71–2, 79, 87, 93, 105, 119

Bellamoure, 113 n.8
Belphoebe, 67, 78, 123–4
Bender, John, 60
Bennett, Josephine Waters, 115 n.37, 116 n.42
Benoît de Sainte-Maure, 47
Berger, Harry, Jr., 14 n.6, 62, 65, 67, 82 nn.10 and 11, 91–4, 95, 113 n.19, 114 nn.24 and 29, 116 n.37
Blatant Beast, 96, 99, 123, 126–29
Boiardo, Matteo Maria, 42
Bono, Barbara, 44–5
Bower of Bliss. *See* Acrasia
Bowra, Maurice, 23
Bradamante, 43, 109
Braggadochio, 126
Bretagne (Brittany, little or lesser Britain), 43, 51 n.4, 113 n.7
Brigants (and cave of), 5, 113 n.8, 127
Britain (Britane, Britany, and Britayne), 3, 6, 8, 13, 25, 29, 42–5, 49–50, 57 n.25, 68, 70, 71–3, 75–6, 80, 85 n.36, 86 n.39, 87–112, 112–3 nn.6 and 7, 113 n.7, 114 n.29, 115 nn.33 and 34, 120, 128. *See also* Celtic; Cornwall; Tudor; Wales
Britannia. *See* Camden, William
Britomart, 6, 45, 50, 53 n.9, 69–70, 71–73, 78, 89, 95, 99–112, 116 n.42, 117 n.48, 119–26
Britomartis, 117 n.48
Briton(s), 3, 6, 12, 61, 62, 71–3, 76, 87–100, 104, 109–10, 114 nn.27 and 30, 120, 124–5, 128
Briton moniments, 89, 92–3, 105–6, 113 n.18
Broceliande, 43
Burbon (Henry IV), 83 n.16, 122
Burghley, William Cecil, Lord, 18 n.20, 29, 128–9
Burrow, Colin, 36 n.14
Busirane (and house of), 5, 64, 102
Butcher, S.H., 35 n.12
Butterfield, H., 36 n.15
Cador, 29, 106
Caelia, 69
Calidore, 6, 50, 72, 94–6, 113 n.8, 114 n.24, 123, 125–7
Calliope, 19
Camden, William, 26, 37 nn.24 and 27, 38 n.31
Campbell, Joseph, 56 n.24
Carme, 108–9, 117 n.48
Carruth, Hayden, 82 n.9
Carthage, 7
Castiglione, Baldassare, 82 n.10
Castle Joyous. *See* Malecasta
Cavalchini, Mariella, 35 n.8
Caxton, William, 48
Celtic, 6, 47, 50, 54 n.16, 85 n.36, 86 n.39, 89, 106
Chanson de Roland, 48
Charlemagne, 42
Chaucer, Geoffrey, 48, 56 n.20, 90, 108–9, 116 nn.42 and 44, 117 nn.45 and 49
Cheney, Donald, 114 nn.27 and 30
Chrétien de Troyes, 47–9, 81–2 n.9
Christ, Jesus. *See* Redcrosse
Chrysogone, 67
Church of England. *See* Reformation
Church, Ralph, 14 n.6
Circle of the Moon, 66
Ciris. *See* Virgil
Claribell, 113 n.8
Cleopolis, 3, 6, 7, 13, 14 n.6, 25, 43, 49–50, 57 n.25, 66, 68, 70, 72, 76–8, 80, 85 n.34, 87–8, 90, 96–7, 100, 106–8, 119–20, 125
Clio, 19, 107
Cocytus, river, 84
Colin Clout, 67, 127
Commendatory Verses (to 1590 *Faerie Queene*), 20, 33–4 nn.1–4
Constantius, 29, 105–6
Contemplation. *See* Mount of
Cook, Albert, 23
Copley, Frank O., 53 n.12
Coridon, 127
Cornwall, 3, 6, 29, 71–2, 86 n.39, 87, 89–90, 106
Cupid, 5, 19, 66, 124, 126
Cyclic Arthuriad (Vulgate Cycle), 47
Cymoent, 5, 66
Cyrus. *See* Xenophon
Daniel, Samuel, 35 n.13
Dante Alighieri, 12, 23, 36 n.14, 73, 79
Dedicatory Sonnets (to 1590 *Faerie Queene*), 39 n.33, 116 n.40
Dee, river, 6, 71, 90
Deneef, A. Leigh, 39 n.35
Descartes, René, 82 n.10
Despair, cave of, 5, 64

Detraction, 99, 123
Devon, 90
Diana, 66–8
Dido, 44–6, 53 n.9
Disdain, 123–4
Divine Comedy. *See* Dante
Dollimore, Jonathan, 15 n.7, 16 n.14
Douglas, Gavin, 56 n.20
Drayton, Michael, 35 n.13
Duessa, 66, 69–70, 77, 79, 83 n.16, 84 n.22, 119–21,
Dunseath, T.K., 14 n.6, 79, 115 n.35
Durling, Robert, 39 n.35, 83 n.16
Eden lands (Eden), 3, 6, 7, 13, 14 n.6, 43, 50, 68–9, 70, 73, 76–8, 80, 87, 96–8, 108, 114 n.27, 119–21
E.K., 33 n.1
Elizabeth I, 18 n.20, 19, 30, 60, 67, 75, 78, 91, 93, 99, 105–8, 122, 124. *See also* Gloriana
Elysium (Elysian), 8, 61, 73
England, 6, 83 n.15, 85 n.31, 89–92, 94, 102, 112 n.6, 113 n.8, 119, 128
Envy, 99, 123
Errour, cave of, 5, 12, 64
Essex, Earl of, 108, 116 n.40
Evans, Robert O., 86 n.39
Eve. *See* Adam
Faerie Queene: 1.Proem, 19–20; 1.9.8–15, 99, 123–4; 1.12.9–11, 77–8; 1.12.17–41, 97–8, 120; 2.Proem, 30–3, 74–5; 2.12.83, 125; 3.1.6–13, 75–6, 111, 126; 3.1.21–3, 121; 3.1.63–6, 111–2; 3.2.8–16, 121; 3.2.17–3.62, 99–112; 3.6.11–29, 66–7; 5.Proem, 74; 5.7.30–45, 121–2; 5.12.26–7, 98–9, 122; 5.12.28–43, 123; 6.7.27–8.30, 123–4; 6.9.3–10.39, 126–7; 6.12.34–41, 127–9
Faery(ies), 6, 13, 62, 90–100, 114 n.27
Faery Court. *See* Cleopolis; Gloriana
Faeryland, 3–8, 19, 30–3, 39 nn.33 and 35, 41–4, 49–50, 51 n.5, 56 n.25, 59–64, 72–6, 79–80, 81 n.4, 82 n.11, 85 n.31, 86 n.39, 87–95, 101–2, 109–12, 114 n.29, 119–21, 125, 127–9
Faery Queen. *See* Gloriana
Fates, 66
Ferguson, Arthur B., 28–9, 36 n.15, 38 nn.28 and 31
Ferguson, Margaret W., 52 n.7
Fichter, Andrew, 14 n.6, 36 n.14, 51 n.1, 52 n.7
Fletcher, Angus, 14 n.6, 84 n.21, 94, 114 n.30
Florimell, 85 n.31, 126
Foucault, Michel, 9
France, 6, 23, 42, 72, 79, 122, 54 n.16
Freud, Sigmund, 15 n.10
Frye, Northrop, 56 n.24, 62, 65, 77, 82 nn.9 and 11, 84 n.24, 86 n.46
Fussner, F. Smith, 27, 36 n.15
Galileo, 82 n.10
Garden of Adonis, 5, 63–4, 67
Gawain (*Gawain and the Green Knight*), 47
Geertz, Clifford, 15 n.7
Geoffrey of Monmouth (*Historia Regum Britanniae*), 26, 48, 115 n.37
Glauce, 69, 87, 100–11, 117 n.48
Gloriana, 3, 6, 7, 19, 26, 29–30, 33 n.2, 49–50, 51 n.5, 66, 69–70, 71, 87–90, 93, 95–9, 106–8, 112, 119–20, 122–25. *See also* Cleopolis
God, 22, 45
Goldberg, Jonathan, 7, 16 n.12, 17 n.19
Golden Age (Saturn's reign), 72–6
Gondibert, 36 n.14
Gorlois, Duke of Cornwall, 71, 87, 117 n.48
Gorre, land of, 81 n.9
Gough, Richard, 37 n.24
Grantorto, 97–8, 122. *See also* Paynims
Gray, Lord. *See* Artegall
Great Britain (British Isles), 87, 89, 113 n.8
Greater Britain. *See* Wales
Greenblatt, Stephen, 8–10, 15 nn.7 and 10, 16 n.12, 17 n.17
Greene, Thomas M., 23, 86 n.46
Greenlaw, Edwin, 26, 37 n.22, 88–9, 91, 93, 112 n.3
Greenlaw, Edwin, et al., *Variorum*, 14 n.6, 115 nn.35 and 37, 116 nn.38 and 42
Gross, Kenneth, 12, 17 n.19
Guillaume de Lorris, 47–8, 54 n.17, 81 n.9
Guyon, 5, 6, 15 n.10, 50, 66, 72, 75, 84 n.22, 93–6, 100, 102, 111, 114 n.24, 121, 125–6
Hades, 5, 63–6, 84 n.22
Hamilton, A.C., 13 n.1, 71, 85 n.32, 86 nn.37, 39, and 49, 115 n.35, 116 n.38

Hankins, John Erskine, 57 n.25, 72, 85 n.34
Hanning, Robert W., 56 n.23
Harding, John, 115 n.37
Harington, John, 51 n.3, 117 n.47
Harper, Carrie A., 115 n.37
Harvey, Gabriel, 20, 33, 56 n.20
Haskins, Charles Homer, 54 n.16
Hathaway, Baxter, 34 n.5
Hawes, Stephen, 56 n.20
Hays, Denys, 36 n.15
Heaven, 63–6, 84 n.24
Helen, 34 n.4
Helgerson, Richard, 10, 15 n.7, 16 n.12, 17 n.18, 21, 36 n.14, 52 n.7, 112 n.6
Hell. *See* Hades
Hera, 70
Herendeen, Wyman H., 37 n.27
Hieatt, A. Kent, 116 n.39
Hill, D.M., 36 n.14
Hobbinol. *See* Harvey, Gabriel
Holinshed, Raphael, 115 n.37
Homer, 4, 20, 21, 30, 33 n.2, 45–6, 53 nn.9 and 11, 79
Horton, Ronald Arthur, 15 n.6, 71, 85 n.36, 86 n.46, 94
Hough, Graham, 57 n.25, 82 n.12, 83 n.15, 91
House of Holiness, 64, 69
Howard, Jean E., 15 n.7, 16 n.13
Hughes, Merritt Y., 56 n.20, 116 nn.42 and 43, 117 n.48
Hulme, Peter, 16 n.14
Hume, Anthea, 15 n.6, 113 n.21
Igrayne, 87
Iliad. *See* Homer
India, 15, 31, 43, 69, 85 n.36
Ireland (land of Irena) 3, 6, 14 n.6, 15 n.10, 38 n.28, 43, 68, 70, 71–3, 79, 85 n.31, 86 n.39, 87, 90, 96–8, 119, 122, 124–5
Isis Church, 5, 63–4, 70, 112
Isle of Man. *See* Lyonesse
Italy, 23, 54 n.16
Ithaca, 4, 7
Iverson, Margaret, 16 n.14
Jacobus de Voragine (*Legenda Sanctorum*), 48
Javitch, Daniel, 34 n.5, 52 n.7
Jean de Meun. *See* Guillaume de Lorris
Jerusalem, 4, 7, 43. *See also* New Jerusalem
Jerusalem Delivered. *See* Tasso, Torquato
Jove (and palace of), 5, 66, 68, 84 n.24, 114 n.27
Kelley, Donald R., 39 n.31
Kellogg, Robert. *See* Scholes, Robert
Kendrick, T.D., 38 n.30
Ker, W.P., 23, 54 n.16
Kermode, Frank, 83 n.16, 85 n.32
Kilcolman Castle, 68
Knights of Maidenhead. *See* Order of Maidenhead
Langland, William, 36 n.14, 48
Latium, 4, 7, 88, 108
Laura, 34 n.2
Lavinia, 45, 53 n.12
Leland, John, 26
Leonardo da Vinci, 82 n.10
Leslie, Michael, 114 n.31
Levine, Joseph M., 38 n.30, 39 n.31
Levy, F.J., 36 n.15
Lewis, C.S., 5, 7, 42, 54 n.17, 63, 64, 67, 80, 81 n.9, 82 nn.12 and 13, 83 n.16
Letter to Ralegh, 4, 5, 11, 13, 14 n.2, 17 nn.19 and 20–1, 23–7, 30, 32–3, 34 n.5, 51 n.1, 53 n.11, 55 n.18, 74–5, 87, 100, 107, 116 n.40, 129
Logris land. *See* England
London. *See* Cleopolis
Lord of Many Islands, 113 n.8
Lucifera, 71
Lydgate, John, 35 n. 13, 48, 56 n.20
Lyonesse, 72, 86 n.39, 109
MacCaffrey, Isabel G., 14 n.6, 60, 62, 63–7, 77, 82 nn.9 and 13, 83 n.16, 84 nn.19, 21, and 22, 94, 95, 113 n.19, 114 n.29, 115 n.35
Machiavelli, Niccolo, 82 n.10
Malecasta, 66, 111, 121
Malengin, cave of, 5, 64
Malory, Thomas, 55 n.18, 57 n.25, 87, 108–9, 112 n.1, 116 n.42, 117 n.46
Mammon (house, cave of), 5, 64, 84 n.22
Manley, Lawrence, 17 n.18
Maresca, Thomas E., 54 n.13, 56 n.24
Marie de France, 47
Marinell, 5, 66, 85 n.31, 126
Mars, 19, 107
Marvell, Andrew, 82 n.10
Mary Stuart. *See* Duessa
McKisack, May, 38 n.30
Medway, river. *See* Thames

Mehl, Dieter, 55 n.19
Meliboe, 113 n.8, 127
Meliogras, 71
Mercilla (and land of), 3, 6, 7, 13, 14 n.6, 68, 70, 78–9, 80, 85 n.34, 87, 93, 119
Merlin, 50, 69, 87, 89, 93, 99–106, 109–10, 116 n.42, 121–2
Miller, Jacqueline T., 17 n.20
Millican, Charles Bowie, 14 n.6, 27, 37 n.22, 71
Milton, John, 53 n.9, 66, 79, 115 n.34
Minos, 108
Mirabella, 123–5
Montrose, Louis A., 10, 16 n.13, 17 n.15
More, Thomas, 82 n.10
Morpheus, house of, 65–6
Morte Darthur. *See* Malory, Thomas
Mount Acidale, 5, 64, 66
Mount of Contemplation, 5, 63–4, 66, 69, 84 n.22, 98, 120–1
Murrin, Michael, 7, 39 n.35, 54 n.13, 72, 80, 83 n.15, 85 n.36, 116 n.41
Mutabilitie, 5, 66, 67–8
Nadel, George F., 34 n.7
Nature, 66, 67, 84 n.24
Nelson, William, 21, 31–2, 39 n.35
New Jerusalem, 5, 94
Night (cave of), 84 n.22
Nohrnberg, James, 14 n.6
O'Connell, Michael, 39 n.32, 110, 113 n.18, 114 n.30
O'Conner, Marion, 16 n.13
Odysseus, 4, 20, 53 n.11
Odyssey. *See* Homer
Order of Maidenhead (Order of the Garter), 73, 95, 101, 114 n.31
Orgoglio (and dungeon of), 5, 64, 99
Orlando Furioso. *See* Ariosto
Orpheus, 20
Osgood, Charles Grosvenor, 85 n.33
Pallas, 46, 53 n.12
Palmer, 75, 96, 126
Paradise Lost. *See* Milton, John
Paris, 4, 7, 43
Parker, M. Pauline, 15 n.6, 83 nn.15 and 16,
Parker, Patricia A., 12, 14 n.6, 57 n.26
Pastorella, 96, 113 n.8, 127
Paynims (and Paynim king), 42, 89, 97, 98–9, 106–7, 114 n.32, 119–20
Pechter, Edward, 15 n.7, 16 n.13
Peru. *See* India
Petrarch, Francesco, 20, 33 n.2
Phaedria (and island of), 85 n.31
Phillip II. *See* Paynims
Pictland, 6, 71, 86 n.39, 113 n.8
Piehler, Paul, 56 n.24
Piers Plowman. *See* Langland, William
Plato, 24, 37 n.21
Pocock, J.G.A., 37 n.26
Ponsonby, William, 27
Proserpina (Garden of), 70, 84 n.22
Proteus (and den of), 85 n.31, 119
Provençal lyric, 54 n.16
Provost, Foster, 83 n.15
Quint, David, 52 n.7
Radigund, 70, 112, 119, 121
Rajan, Balachandra, 18 n.22
Ralegh, Walter, 17 n.19, 20, 29, 33 n.2. *See also* Letter to Ralegh
Rathborne, Isabel E., 14 n.6, 60–1, 73–4, 85 n.36, 93, 94, 114 n.29, 116 n.38
Redcrosse, 5, 6, 7, 50, 66, 69, 71–2, 77–8, 89–90, 93–100, 106, 108, 110–1, 119–21, 123, 125
Reformation, 15 n.10, 76–8, 96–7. *See also* Eden lands
Richards, I.A., 84 n.19
Roche, Thomas P., Jr., 7, 73, 79–80, 91–2, 116 n.43, 117 nn.48 and 50
Roland, 42
Roman de la Rose. *See* Guillaume de Lorris
Romantic, 12
Rome (and Romans), 4, 44, 88, 89, 108, 116 n.39. *See also* Augustan; Paynims
Rome, Church of. *See* Duessa; Paynims
Rosalind, 20
Ruggiero, 43, 109
Ryence, 71, 87, 104, 106, 110, 117 n.48
St. Bernard, 46–7
St. Francis, 47
St. George. *See* Redcrosse
Salvage Knight. *See* Artegall
Samient, 79
Samuel, Irene, 35 n.8
Sansjoy, 66
Saracens. *See* Paynims
Satan, 53 n.9, 77–8
Satyrane, 69, 122
Saxon(s), 6, 87, 89, 104, 109, 110, 115 n.32

Scholes, Robert (and Robert Kellogg), 60, 63, 115 nn.33 and 34
Scorn, 123
Scotland. *See* Pictland
Scylla, 108–9, 117 n.48
Serena, 128
Severn, river, 6, 71, 90
Shakespeare, William, 35 n.12, 102, 82 n.10
Shepheardes Calender, 33
Sidney, Philip, 20; *Arcadia*, 35 n.13, 36 n.14, 82 n.10; *Defence of Poesie*, 23–5, 27–8, 37 nn.16, 21, and 27, 129
Sinfield, Alan, 10, 16 n.14
Southern, R.W., 54 n.15
Spain, 97
Spingarn, J.E., 34 n.5
Squire's Tale. *See* Chaucer
Steadman, John M., 52 n.9
Stevens, John, 56 n.24
Stow, John, 115 n.37
Strachy, James, 15 n.10
Suzuki, Mihoko, 53 n.9
Tale of Sir Thopas. *See* Chaucer
Talus, 75, 97–8, 122–3
Tamar, river, 6, 71, 90
Tanaquill. *See* Gloriana
Tasso, Torquato: *Gerusalemme Liberata*, 4, 11, 22, 30, 33, 41–4, 51 n.1, 52 n.7, 79–80,; *Discourses on the Heroic Poem*, 21–2, 35 nn.8–11, 96
Temple of Venus, 5, 64, 67
Teskey, Gordon, 11–12, 56 n.26
Thames (and Medway), river, 85 n.31, 90
Tiber, river, 69
Tillyard, E.M.W., 7, 8–9, 15 n.8, 23, 35 nn.9, 12, and 13, 56 nn.20 and 25, 116 n.41
Timias, 123, 128
Timon, 87, 99
Tristram, 71–2, 87, 108–9, 117 n.46
Troilus, 117 n.45
Troy (and Trojans and Trojan War), 4, 7, 21, 46
Troynovant. *See* Cleopolis
Tudor (line, myth, prophecy, apocalypse) 6, 7, 10, 19, 26–30, 59, 78, 88, 89–92, 97, 105–8, 119, 128, 129
Turnus, 46, 53 n.12
Tuve, Rosemond, 63, 83 n.18, 102
Tweed, river, 6, 71, 113 n.8
Ulysses. *See* Odysseus
Una, 7, 50, 68–9, 70, 76–7, 98, 99, 106, 108, 120–1, 123–5
Upton, John, 14 n.6
Uther Pendragon, 29, 73, 87, 104–6, 117 n.48
Venus, 19, 66–7, 70, 126
Vesser, H. Aram, 16 n.13
View of the Present State of Ireland, 28, 38 n.28
Vinaver, Eugene, 55 n.18
Virgil: *Aeneid*, 4, 19, 20, 21–2, 30, 36 n.14, 44–6, 53 nn.9 and 12, 54 n.13, 73, 88, 108, 120; *Ciris*, 108–9, 116 n.43, 117 n.48
Virgil, Polydore, 26–7
Virginia. *See* India
Wales (North and South), 3, 6, 7, 14 n.6, 51 n.4, 71, 86 n.39, 89–90, 99, 104–6, 113 n.7, 119, 123. *See also* Britain
Waller, Gary, 15 n.9
Weinberg, Bernard, 34 n.5
Williams, Kathleen, 82 n.9, 115 n.35
Wind, Edgar, 84 n.19
Woolf, D.R., 36 n.15, 38 n.30, 39 n.31
Xenophon, 24–5, 37 n.21

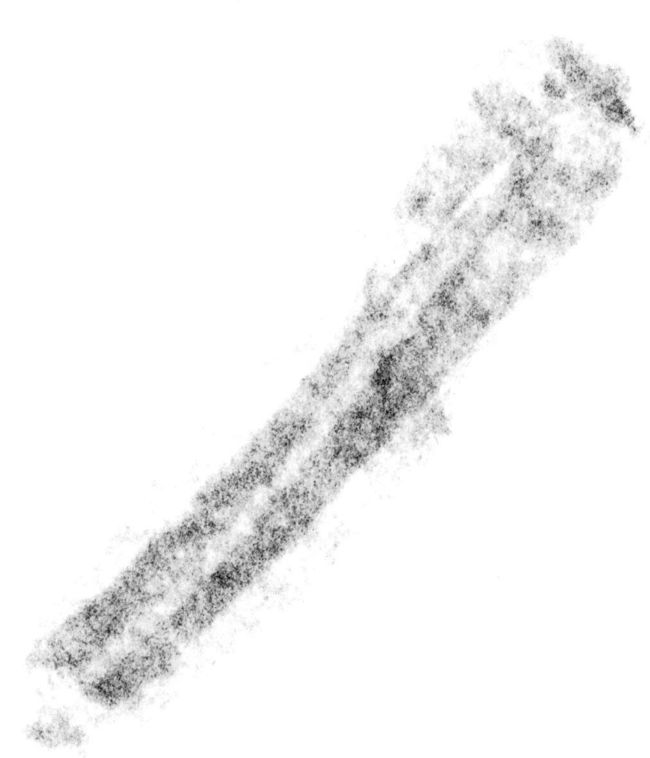